CAN'T BUY HEALTH

Book 1

Author's Foreword

This is the first part of a new series that languished on my old laptop for several years while the stars of the Sax Man series, and the Football Crazy series, took over. Interestingly, a version of it was my first ever book produced back in my teenage years as a result of a newspaper promotion - collect the tokens and pay a certain amount to have your book printed and 4 copies.

I have been challenged to write, and publish, 50 books in my lifetime. Currently, I have plans and basic outlines, and most have a first draft, for 41 of those 50 (!) Nuts, huh? I have every intention of fulfilling the challenge. With a decrease in my mental and physical health, there are plans in place to help me achieve it.

For the start of the new series, I have chosen a date that is very special to those of us who knew my good friend Laura. She gained her angel wings suddenly and without warning last month, and this publication date is the day we get to say our final goodbyes. The title of the series, Can't Buy Health, is hugely apt for a lot of us.

Yvonne

Chapter 1

"I can't take any more," Yvette whispered, shaking her head, on the edge of tears.

"Yes you can, Eve." Austin's tone was one of patience and calm, as it usually was.

She sniffed back her tears. "No Aus, I don't live a day without painkillers..."

"I know my darling, but it takes time."

Continuing to shake her head, more tears slid down Yvette's face. "I'll never recover... I'll need stronger and stronger drugs, until they're so strong they knock me out all the time."

Austin stopped the thread of his argument, knowing what she had said was true. Gradually a dose of painkillers wore off, having minimal then no effect on her, then the dosage increased. Unsurprisingly, alongside this, Yvette's dislike of doctors heightened.

Yet common sense told him there was a cure somewhere... or at least something that would ease her suffering. Surely?

Soothing her back to sleep, he returned to their latest work. That was one sign Yvette was feeling more like herself, her passion for words was slowly returning. Also, she had agreed to the plan that they would write together.

"...can't go on like this..." She sobbed, her head buried into his chest.

"My poor darling." Austin had Yvette wrapped his arms, kissing her sore head gently.

It seemed she couldn't stop repeating herself – it hurts: Austin was trying not to let it get to him, but struggling to deal with her pain and his own.

As good as it felt to be held close to him, the feelings of frustration and surrender to the ever present pain never subsided. Yvette wept, only inflaming the pain she struggled with.

Austin shook his head, snapping back to reality, the dream still haunting him. Normality was a headache: he wondered what he'd do if Yvette told him one day she didn't have one. It wasn't doing much to improve her temperament either: he sighed.

Of all of life's importance, why was it not possible to buy health? Anyone with money could buy virtually anything they wanted – anything but the component of good health.

Realising they were fortunate to have their friends around, he sighed again. Every so often he needed time out and Jack and Zoe helped in many ways, giving him peace of mind for the short time he was absent from Yvette's side.

Yet... the guilt ate at him. Every time he left her, did it make things worse? Did he cause her more suffering by leaving? Mentally he scolded himself, thinking like this would do neither of them any good. He knew Yvette was fine with Zoe for a while.

They both enjoyed getting together: Zoe managed to distract her friend to the point where she felt better within herself. It was silly to worry that she wouldn't be able to cope without him, especially when he wouldn't be gone long.

Kissing Yvette before he went, he squeezed Zoe's shoulder on his way out. They'd be fine, there was nothing to worry about. By looking into her eyes, he could tell if Yvette was suffering more than usual, or not. It was safe to leave for a while, she was fine.

Sometimes he had to get out: Yvette was his everything but without some alone-time he'd go mad. He couldn't help but feel their lives were wasting away.

Jack and Zoe had a normal life - jobs, kids, happiness... and all the bills and worry to boot. Austin sighed again. But there was nothing that could be done, no-one knew how long it would be until Yvette recovered; come to think of it, no-one knew what it was exactly. Her health fluctuated so much.

They were nearly in their thirties, what a thought! Yes, they had no bills to worry about, thanks to Yvette's writing history had become so legendary. He smiled with the thought of his dear, sweet Yvette. His stomach flipped at the thought of what could've been, but he pushed the dreams out of his head:

'Yvette wouldn't have liked all the publicity, she prefers the quiet life.'

And a quiet life was certainly what she had. What they had, he corrected himself.

Between his sport-associated injuries and Yvette's declining health, he hadn't lasted long on a professional pitch, so nobody truly knew how much he could have achieved. Every manager who had witnessed his play remarked on his natural talent, even in the early days...

Austin shook his head to dismiss the thoughts.

They needed a break: getting away would do them both good - ah, now there was a thought, their Cornwall retreat! It had been years since they'd been down there. The sound of the sea, the call of the birds, the smell of the fresh sea air - Yvette would love it. His smile widened...

The screeching of tyres snapped him from his daydream.

"Oh my God! Are you alright?" A young woman got out of the car, hurrying to him and kneeling beside him, where he'd sunk to the tarmac in shock. Literally, she had stopped the car not more than a half an inch from him. "I didn't hurt you, did I?" She was shaking as she touched his arm gently.

Austin gathered his scattered wits, shaking his head. "It's okay, I'm alright."

Reversing out of the driveway, she hadn't seen him because of the high bushes at either side of the gateposts. Austin hadn't seen her car coming either, again the bushes at fault.

"I told you to be more careful! You drive too fast, Elisabeth!" Another voice chastised the young woman then. "Let's get him inside. Can you walk, young man?" An older woman appeared beside them, her attention focused on Austin once her initial worry that there had been an accident had been unfounded.

"I'm fine, honestly." He tried, but his protest was in vain.

"Have a sit down inside, and we'll see how you are." The older woman continued.

Heart pounding, Austin gave in and got shakily to his feet. They both helped walk him into the house and made him sit down on the sofa.

"How are you feeling?" Elisabeth stayed by his side, concern written all over her face. The other lady, referred to as Susan, bustled away again to make them all tea.

Austin took a deeper breath. "Not so good, actually." He admitted, unable to control the shaking; it seemed to be getting worse, and now he was going lightheaded. He recognised the signs - his blood sugar had fallen, no doubt due to the shock of their near-miss. He tried not to groan aloud.

"I've made us a nice cuppa." Susan was back, a laden tea tray in her hand.

"I think he needs some sugar, that was a nasty fright." Elisabeth suggested, her own heart still pounding over the incident.

Austin swallowed, trying to find his voice. "I'm diabetic..."

"Diabetic?" Susan repeated. "I've got just the thing, hang on. Elisabeth, keep an eye on him. I'll be back soon."

The horrid sensation of his every muscle tensing signalled that he was going to be ill. And he wanted Yvette: it was his immediate reaction when he was unwell.

"Have you any medication with you?" She asked hopefully, the realisation dawning on her that they weren't out of trouble yet.

Sweat gathered on his brow. "No, I only came out for a short walk." Austin leant back against the softness of the plump sofa cushions, closing his eyes.

"You need to drink this." Susan placed a glass of dark fizzing liquid into his shaky hand.

"What is it?" Elisabeth frowned. "Susan, you cannot expect him to drink something he doesn't know..."

"Cola, my dear, best thing for him."

Her frown deepened. "Are you sure?"

Susan nodded, encouraging him to drink.

Slowly Austin took in the liquid, willing the cure to work. Although he hadn't used the trick before, he had heard of it being used to stave off the worst of a hypoglycaemic attack. He also took several deep breaths.

"Now while I'll bring you a refill, tell Elisabeth where you live and what your name is so that we can phone your wife."

"No!" Austin turned a paler shade of white. "Don't ring her, for God's sake." He took a slow deep breath, feeling badly in need of a lie down.

The image of Yvette's frightened expression when she found out he had fallen ill swam in front of him when he closed his eyes.

"Is there anyone else we can call?" Elisabeth questioned him as Susan left once more.

Austin shook his head, opening his eyes again. "No." He paused, while his thoughts raced along with his heart rate. "She's ill - I look after her. I have to get back."

Sorrowfully, and more than a little horrified, Elisabeth shook her head.

"You can't have left her alone? Who is with your wife now?" Susan continued, bustling back into the room, and the conversation.

"A friend… but I don't want her leaving Yvette."

Both women nodded.

"I'll take you home," Elisabeth said, "it's the least I can do. Is it far?"

She nodded at the directions he gave her, glad that it wasn't too far away.

Chapter 2

"Aus?" Zoe called, hearing the door open.

She was in the kitchen, giving Yvette peace to sleep. Watching the time, she'd started to worry as Austin had been gone longer than he'd said. Going to find him when she didn't hear his footsteps coming to her, she traced him and a stranger to the lounge.

"Austin! Oh my God, what happened?" Zoe's heart leapt into her mouth, leaning over to hug him as her automatic instinct told her.

Elisabeth hovered awkwardly at their side. "I...well ...we nearly had an accident. We've kept an eye on him, he was adamant he was fine, but I'm not sure."

Zoe rolled her eyes. "That sounds like him." One look into his deathly pale face told her that he truly wasn't right: her heart began pounding afresh. "Aus, I'm gonna call the doctor. Hang on." Looking up at their guest, she asked her to stay at least until their doctor had been.

Elisabeth agreed, guilt mounting as they were left alone again.

Zoe was soon back. "Won't be long Aus, you'll be alright. I've brought your medication."

Austin nodded, taking it from her.

Zoe grimaced and turned away, unable to watch as he injected himself. She turned to Elisabeth, who was feeling more and more uncomfortable, asking her what happened. So Elisabeth unravelled the tale, apologising profusely as she talked.

"It's not your fault. Accidents happen." Zoe smiled gently at the stranger.

"Zoe..."

Her attention returned to Austin as he spoke her name, very quietly. "Aus, it's okay. C'mere." She cuddled him again, feeling him shaking, glad that he was still able to inject himself. That was a good sign, she knew.

He whispered in her ear, silently praying. "Is Eve..."

"Eve's fast asleep, don't worry, she's okay." She rubbed his back comfortingly. "You'll be alright. I'll look after you."

"We didn't know what to do." Elisabeth had a handkerchief in her hands and was twisting it worriedly in her lap.

Zoe looked up at her, giving her a kind smile. "You did great. I only want to have him checked over, in case."

At that exact moment, there came a soft knocking followed by some footsteps in the hall. It wasn't their usual doctor, but that didn't matter: any medical professional would know what to do.

Elisabeth related the tale again as the doctor carried out his checks. Soon he disappeared, satisfied with his patient's condition, but warning that if he worsened, they needed to get him to the hospital. Elisabeth made her excuses to leave once the doctor had, desperate to get away from the nightmare scenario.

Zoe thanked and reassured her as she let her out, returning to Austin as quickly as she could. Finding him asleep on the sofa, she felt his forehead, relieved that he wasn't cold and clammy – a sign that he would be needing further medical attention.

Heaving a sigh of relief, she went then to check on Yvette, her relief doubling when she saw she was still sleeping. The last thing she wanted to do was upset her, especially knowing Austin would soon recover.

Sitting with him in the lounge, she watched over him until he woke up, keeping half an eye on the monitor showing

Yvette sleeping also.

When Yvette awoke later that afternoon, both Zoe and Austin were sitting with her. As her eye fell on Austin's pale face, she patted the bed beside her, indicating that he should lie down and cuddle into her.

Austin did as he was bade, sighing as her arms went around him. His earlier instinct had been right, he did feel better cuddled in close to her.

Yvette smiled, catching Zoe's eye and pulling a face. Zoe nodded and Yvette nodded in return. She knew Austin wasn't right, despite him not saying anything, and silently squeezed him. Their silent communication with Zoe proved their theories were the same. He would be fine, given time.

Zoe spoke then, convinced that it was safe to leave the pair for a while. "I'll go now, but I'll come back this evening once the kids are in bed."

"Okay, thanks Zoe." Yvette smiled at her, nodding at the silent instruction to phone if she was needed. Zoe smiled and kissed her friend's cheek, then Austin's, before she left.

Austin smiled and also kissed Yvette, cuddling as close to her as he could.

"Rest honey," she told him, returning his kiss.

Without argument Austin did as he was told, gratefully sinking into sleep with Yvette by his side. As he did, his mind was on his earlier idea to get away for a while.

Chapter 3

It was the first time in months there had been any contact between the friends since Yvette and Austin had escaped to Cornwall for their break.

Fatefully, while they had been away from home, Yvette's health had taken a dramatic turn for the worst. It seemed the headaches that had plagued her for months had been a warning sign. Once released from the hospital back to their Cornish dwelling, Austin had refused anyone entry, except Thirza, their hired help.

He had been advised against taking her home to their city life, for many reasons; this was why having Thirza was necessary – they knew nobody here, and as much as Austin hated the idea of needing help, he couldn't deny the need was desperate.

Slowly, Yvette was starting to improve; painfully slowly. Hence his agreement to Jack's offer of a visit. Until now, everything had been communicated via sporadic messaging between Austin and his friends. Sudden, shrill noises affected Yvette for the worst, and Austin would never let anything, no matter how small and seemingly insignificant, harm her further... including phone calls, either voice or video.

For weeks, he had delayed answering their friends' questions about visiting. As much as he wanted to have their support, and thought Yvette too would benefit now she was improving, it all added more strain for him.

The pair had children, although both were old enough to know to keep quiet when asked and knew that Auntie Yvette was very ill. That too had to be taken into consideration; not to mention how Zoe would react when she saw Yvette. He knew because he had done it: Zoe would be the same mix of horrified and over emotional, he knew.

When Jack had come up with the compromise of visiting alone, Austin had hesitated. His friend was brave to put himself into the position of seeing them for the first time after Yvette's collapse alone, and Austin appreciated the gesture. Even after agreeing, and laying down some necessary ground rules, Austin changed his mind about the idea several times as Jack's journey south had begun...

That night, Jack arrived so late it was pitch black. Parking on the gravel beside the house, he stepped out of the car and stretched. Fresh sea air hit him the moment he got out: automatically he breathed it in deeply.

What a difference from the choking London smog! It was no wonder the doctors had all advised that the pair remain in the fresh coastal climate: the health benefits were many. Remembering Austin's instructions, Jack took several calming deep breaths before walking up to the door to knock gently.

Finally, he got an answer. It worried him how long it took, especially as Austin knew of his expected time of arrival. But he didn't have time to think any more of the thought - his heart sank when he saw his friend: Austin's skeletal frame and white hair only enhanced the image the descriptive word created. It certainly was apt.

Frozen in shock, Jack stood where he was, rooted to the spot, his tongue tied.

"Come in for goodness sake." Austin ushered him into the house, shutting the door quietly but firmly behind them.

"Sorry Aus." Jack snapped himself out of it, putting his bag down to hug him. "It's good to see you."

"I must look a fright," Austin half-laughed, "judging by your face."

Jack shook his head, trying to dislodge his horror. "How's things?"

They parted and Austin shrugged. He didn't know how to answer the question, if indeed there was an answer. Jack knew that it was a dangerous question to ask, but nonetheless one that he felt compelled to ask.

Following him through to the main bedroom, Jack paused at the door. Yvette was so much worse, she made Austin look normal. Drifting into the room, automatically he sat down.

"Not that side," Austin spoke gently, "this is her good side."

Jack mentally kicked himself, remembering too late what Austin had told him. Yvette had recovered feeling on one side of her body, but she couldn't talk; her only communication was via hand squeezes.

His horror, far from subsiding, increased. No way was Zoe coming. She couldn't see Yvette like this! He had to protect her...

Suddenly a shrillness broke the air - his phone.

"Oh God, sorry!" The words were out before he could hold them back.

Seeing it was Zoe he decided against turning it off, instead leaving the room quickly to answer the call. Yvette's face contorted with pain he saw as he left: he swore to himself.

"I was... Jack, are you alright?"

The screen was so clear Zoe could read Jack's expressions and actions like she was there: he looked like he'd seen a ghost, or worse.

"I'm okay." His face broke into a smile at her concern. "The drive was alright, the roads are much quieter at this time."

His expression changed again as Yvette's pained moans reached his ear. "That was bad timing, Zoe. I'll have to turn the phone off while I'm here. Eve's not good."

"What d'you mean, not good?" Zoe's voice dropped to a whisper.

Jack was shaking his head, not knowing where to begin. It was far worse than he'd been preparing himself for, he had to admit.

Horror cascaded over her. She'd known it was bad, long before Austin had agreed to the visit. All of Zoe's senses screamed at her to be there: Yvette needed her, and Austin too would need help. She was thankful they had Thirza, but still, nobody would be as good as she was.

"I'm coming down, I have to..." Zoe began.

"No Zoe." Jack's tone shut off her argument. "You can't see her, not like this. Aus was right, you'll be too upset."

Zoe was stunned into silence.

"I'm... I'm not sure I can do it myself." He felt his emotion rise, barely managing to get the words out.

"Jack… Jack!" Zoe's helplessness increased seeing his upset.

"You and your bloody phone!" Austin exploded.

As he neared his friend, he realised two things simultaneously: Jack was in tears and Zoe was staring right back at him from the screen, her expression one of absolute horror. This was the first time she had seen Austin as well.

Mentally, he prepared himself for the barrage of questions from the pair. Taking the phone from Jack's hand, Austin plugged it into his laptop and flipped up the screen Adjusting the volume so that it wasn't too loud, because he had the bedroom door open to allow Yvette to hear where he was, and give him as few obstacles as possible to get back to her.

"Aus..." Zoe found her voice first.

"I know." Austin cut her off. He took several deep breaths, trying to quash the notion that he shouldn't have involved the pair. "This is why we stayed down here. It was easier, and I didn't want you two involved. There's enough upset and unrest here as it is. I'm sorry if that's not what you want to hear."

"I'm so sorry, I couldn't..." Jack began.

"I expected it. Now you know what it's been like." He blew his breath out. "Eve's... torture has almost torn us apart. Bless her," he half smiled, "she's so far out of it she doesn't know what's happened." His voice trailed off sadly.

Zoe kicked herself, wishing she was there to help and comfort their friends.

Jack moved then, putting his arm around his mate's shoulders. "We're here,"

"For both of you." Zoe finished. She allowed a silence to develop before she continued. "Thank you Aus, you had our best interest at heart."

Austin let out a shaky sigh. "You can see her, when she's better. The doctors reckon she's strengthening now." He paused, taking more deep breaths. "I'm sorry, I just couldn't handle anything else. Yvette always comes first."

Zoe and Jack were nodding. They knew that was his way of thinking.

"Is she okay? I mean, she will be okay, won't she?" Zoe held her breath, slowly letting it go again. "I had to ask." She replied to Jack's eye-rolling. "I'm stuck here worrying, I have to know." Her bottom lip trembled as tears slipped down her face.

Austin shook his head. "I don't know. We can't tell."

He took another few breaths, long and deep, trying to rearrange the words in his mind to make some sort of sense.

The medical terminology went straight over his head, but the specialist had given him a basic translation.

"Something inside shut down and refused to come up again."

"But why?!" Zoe wailed, tears streaming down her face.

Instantly Jack tried to console her, wishing for a moment that they were together.

"Zoe, listen." Austin pulled himself together, her grief awakening his. "Deep breaths, alright? Someone very special is watching over us. They saved her and returned Yvette to us. We must be strong - Yvette needs us."

Zoe nodded, almost pulling herself together in the next few minutes.

Nodding to himself, Austin made his decision. "I'm going to check on her, I'll leave you two to talk. But please, Zoe, if you want to phone, let us know first."

His friends both nodded as he got up, still sitting in a shocked silence as he left the room.

Closing the bedroom door over behind him, Austin sighed deeply. There was enough to deal with without those two making things worse. Of course they would be shocked and upset, he had to give them some kind of leeway - but they had to be strong for Yvette. It was still possible she'd... No! He wasn't going to think that way.

From here, it was difficult to tell whether she was asleep or not. As he neared the bed, her hand twitched. She was aware of things around her, and definitely of his presence. No doubt she had heard his sigh, and was wondering what it meant.

"Eve, I'm here sweetheart." He made his way directly to her. He kissed the back of her good hand; something which always made her smile - he missed that, he realised then. "Don't worry Eve, it's alright. Jack's here to see us, and he's talking to Zoe at the moment. I've just been to say a few things." - Was it his imagination, or did Yvette's face pall? - "They're gonna help us as much as they can. Zoe will be here when you're better."

He could imagine her smile, knowing that it would come in time... In time, but not soon enough to his mind.

Fifteen or so minutes later, Jack came back in quietly, and somewhat sheepishly. Seeing movement in Yvette's face, almost as if she was wincing... repeatedly wincing, her eyes tightly closed: his heart pounded.

"What do I do?" He asked softly.

"Open the window, and keep quiet." Austin instructed.

Jack took offence from his tone, but Austin had other things on his mind: sitting upright on the bed against the pillows, taking Yvette into his arms. Involuntarily, intermittently, she was whimpering.

Austin squeezed his eyes closed in concentration, listening and hoping. Silently, he was thankful that Jack had followed his request and was keeping quiet. And then, there it was... that magical sound.

All of a sudden, Jack could hear it too. The sound of the sea; gentle waves lapping on the beach. Austin prayed that Yvette too was hearing it: the magical sound got through to her, seeming to unexplainably revive her.

Jack didn't dare move. They stayed like that for hours, until, suddenly, he came out of his trance-like state, realising both Austin and Yvette were fast asleep.

What the hell happened? He shook his head; even racking his brain, he didn't know. What did he do now - did he stay here, or did he find the spare room? He left Austin a note, in large print so that he could read it from where he was, informing him of his decision to retire to the spare room.

Chapter 4

Her eyes, now open, focused slowly.

Austin...

She knew Austin would be there; he promised he would always be with her. As he'd told her; as he promised; he was right beside her. She knew she could rely on him to keep his promise.

"Aus..." Her voice sounded so weak and feeble.

Austin woke up because of her tight grip on his hand. Once he realised, his face lit up: this was one of the promising signs he was told to look out for.

"Yvette?" His voice was excited, but he tried to keep his tone soft.

Her reply was a smile: a small smile, but a huge achievement in terms of the start of her recovery.

"Yvette! My sweet, brave Yvette!" Stroking her face and hair tenderly, he couldn't help his massive, excited grin. "Eve, you did speak, didn't you? No, don't try again, save your energy. Just squeeze my hand once if you did."

She again squeezed his hand, but not quite as tightly as she had done to wake him.

"Oh Yvette!" Tears trickled down his face.

Squeezing his hand again, she could feel... she was actually feeling the wetness from her tears slipping down her cheeks.

The light was getting through, although the room seemed dark. She was confused ...and it was tiring, all this. Her eyelids felt heavy: she couldn't keep them open much longer, no matter how much she wanted to stay awake, the pull was too strong to resist.

"It's okay sweetheart, you need lots of rest. I'll be here

when you wake up, I promise. Let yourself rest." He reassured her, watching as she succumbed to sleep, no more than a few seconds later.

Hours later, Austin was beaming when he contacted Zoe and Jack: their doctor had confirmed her improvements, also drawing up Yvette's recovery plan.

Exhausted after her assessment, her threshold holding for no longer than three minutes, Yvette knew that was a lifetime more than she'd had for months...

It would come, the doctor had told them, and Austin repeated this to her as she slept again. He praised her, whispering salutations of his love for her as she succumbed once more.

As the school summer holidays approached, the family planned to visit their friends in Cornwall. It would be the first time that Zoe would get to see Yvette, an urge that had strengthened since Jack's solo visit four months ago.

With news of Yvette's continuing improvement, Zoe couldn't help thinking it was an omen – both for their visit and Yvette's future. They had barely dropped their belongings at the hotel before she was on the phone to arrange their visit.

Austin gave her a kind smile, pointing out what she already knew in her heart. "There's no point coming over tonight, Eve's out for the count now. Morning will be best."

This made sense, but Zoe felt disappointed... but so relieved Yvette was through. She blinked back the tears in her eyes. They all knew that she was a fighter: how she had battled back from the awful accident that had left her paralysed some years ago proved it.

But sometimes the decision wasn't yours to make, they knew. The human body could be a very strange thing.

Sending prayers up to their angel, Zoe had been doing this with regularity in the last few months, she also gave thanks.

It was a beautiful location being this close to the sea: it was no wonder Austin and Yvette had fallen in love with their beach front property. Fortunately, the kids - Tom and Kim - were old enough to amuse themselves and would be perfectly safe within view of their friends' house, so this meant she could have Yvette to herself.

At least, while Jack distracted Austin. Zoe wasn't entirely sure that Austin would leave Yvette's side, but that didn't matter. Despite their long and tiring journey, she could barely sleep that night.

Letting themselves in as Austin had arranged, they went quietly through the house, Jack showing Zoe through to the master bedroom where their friends were.

Austin had Yvette sitting up in bed, resting back against him. He was nice and warm and comforting; so much so, Yvette wouldn't move for the world. Zoe couldn't help dissolving into tears when she saw her friend.

"Sshh, she's just dropping off." Austin whispered, aware that company had arrived.

Quietly Zoe came across to them, reaching out to stroke Yvette's hair.

Yvette murmured, stirring slightly.

"Sshhh..." Zoe shushed her. "You sleep babe, we'll be here when you wake."

"Z..o..e..." Yvette tried to fight the tiredness, she couldn't open her eyes but she reached out with her good arm for her friend.

"Sshh, sleep babe. You need lots of rest." Zoe smiled as Yvette found her arm and fell asleep at the same time. She tried to swallow the lump in her throat, glad when Jack put his arms comfortingly around her.

Yvette could hear the three around her, their voices were quite clear but she couldn't fight it; gradually the voices muffled, and disappeared as the blackness took her over.

Chapter 5

Months later...

"Austin, I'm so sorry, I don't know where to go." Zoe burst into tears when he opened the door to her.

It had just gone three in the morning when the doorbell woke him. Amazingly, it didn't wake Yvette: checking the security camera, he was astonished to see Zoe standing there, shivering in only a soggy t-shirt.

Pouring rain coupled with the freezing October wind whipping up a gale made even Austin shiver. Putting his arm around her shoulders, drawing her inside, closing and locking the door behind them, he was suddenly wide awake. Taking her into the lounge, so that their voices wouldn't disturb Yvette, he went with his instinct to comfort her.

"Oh Zoe, c'mere." He hugged her.

Zoe yelped, clutching her side.

Immediately he let her go. "What's wrong?"

"He... he hit me, Aus." She sank onto the sofa.

"He what?!" Anger rose in Austin's voice.

"...don't..." More tears slipped down her face. "Please Aus, don't be mad at me."

"Zoe." He softened his tone, sitting beside her, wanting to hug her but not wanting to hurt her further. "Zoe, I'm not mad at you. What happened?"

Zoe buried her head in her hands. Her silence spoke volumes.

"It's okay Zoe, you're safe here. We'll look after you." Gently he took her nearest hand in his. "I'd hug you, but I don't want to cause you more pain."

She nodded. "It's this side,"

Austin switched sides. "So from here, it's alright?"

She nodded and he half-hugged her from the opposite side.

A thought struck him - the kids. "Did you...?"

She nodded, cutting him off. "Kicked me out, threw my bag at me and..."

- That explained the car then.

"Came back late, drunk, and... went mental..." Her voice broke completely then.

In the next moment, she pulled away from him and half-ran out of the room. Austin was puzzled, until he heard her retching.

Tracking her down, he found her crumpled on the bathroom floor, crying and trying to catch her breath. Turning the heat on with a small click, he wrapped a towel around her shoulders, making her drink a glass of water when she was a bit calmer.

Talking to her comfortingly and soothingly, much as he did with Yvette, he was relieved when she calmed.

"C'mon, let's get you out of those wet clothes and into a nice hot shower, eh?" He smiled kindly at her, glad that she was regaining her self control.

Zoe groaned. "Is Eve okay? I didn't disturb her as well, did I?"

"No, don't worry. Eve's well out for the count." He looked worriedly as Zoe grimaced and held her side again. "See if you can get out of that wet soggy mess and into the shower, I'll go'n get you some dry clothes."

Zoe nodded, trying to summon her strength while he was gone. She knew he wouldn't be long, looking up as he returned.

"I haven't got the energy," she whispered. She hadn't

moved at all since he'd left.

"I'll help you, if you want?" He offered.

Zoe nodded.

Austin removed the towel from around her and helped her to sit up. "Tell me what hurts? I don't want to hurt you any more. Just point, save your energy."

Having cared for Yvette for so long certainly came in use. Undressing her down to underwear, they then moved across to the shower unit. Zoe sat as she was told to on the seat inside the shower.

"I'll adjust the water, then you can take it from there, alright?"

She nodded, not even having the strength to be embarrassed about him having to take her clothes off for her. They had known each other a very long time, but even so.

He decided it was best not to totally strip her off, not knowing what frame of mind she was in. Always best to play safe. But he did notice her bruises: many, and at different stages of healing, which meant several incidents. His inner rage rose, but he knew for all of their sakes, he had to contain it.

A short while later Zoe emerged, feeling a little better. Apologising quietly for making him jump, she smiled slightly at his dismissal.

"Are you okay?"

She nodded at his question, then shrugged.

"D'you want a drink, or something to eat, or just go to bed?"

She took in a shaky breath. "I wanna go to bed... but I....I can't. I'm..."

"Too frightened?"

Zoe nodded, fresh tears rolling down her face.

He offered her another hug, careful not to squeeze her bruised side. "You're safe here, Zoe. I'll look after you, you know that." He got her to nod, unsure of where her thoughts were. "I'll have to get you checked."

Zoe looked up, horrified.

Austin saw her expression, and explained. "I'm worried about your ribs, they're black and blue. I don't suppose you've taken any painkillers?"

Slowly, Zoe shook her head.

"I'll give you some; we have plenty here!" Austin was glad his lightheartedness made her smile. He quickly returned with some, and a glass of chilled juice.

Zoe looked questioningly at the purple liquid.

"Eve loves blackcurrant, it's all we have, sorry. I hope that's okay?"

She nodded and smiled, gratefully taking it from him and swallowing the pills. "I'm sorry Aus, I'm keeping you up."

Austin shrugged. "I'm used to it with Eve."

"How is she?"

The atmosphere changed noticeably. He was carefully considering his answer, she realised.

"She's okay, most days, but sometimes she has these little ...fits."

"Fits?" Zoe repeated.

Austin nodded. "She'll moan, shake, cry - it's totally out of her control. She has no warning, and most of the time she isn't aware of what she's doing."

Zoe was shocked.

"They're getting less all the time now, thank God." He continued.

Zoe nodded, feeling tired now. At last, she was able to relax, knowing she was safe here. Austin was right, she knew she was safe here: that was why she had made the long drive down to the coast. Soon, she was asleep on Austin's shoulder.

Austin sighed, anger welling up inside him. Even if he was drunk, what right did that give Jack for hitting poor Zoe? How much had she suffered? Austin clenched his fists - had he been abusing the kids as well as his wife?

Their doctor was scheduled to see Yvette tomorrow, and Zoe could be checked over as well, but they'd have to involve the police. There was no way that Jack was going to get away with this.

Gently he laid Zoe down where they were on the sofa, fetching a blanket to drape over her. The rain had eased and the street was quiet. Austin smiled to himself, the street was normally quiet, that was the beauty of this place.

Chapter 6

Days later, the kids had been moved down to Cornwall with Zoe, Austin and Yvette, where it was deemed a safe environment after Zoe's police interview. Austin felt it was better for all of them, and reassured Zoe that there was plenty of room for them all.

A week later, Zoe felt able to see Jack in order to talk as the specialists had advised, but only with Yvette and Austin present. The old saying of safety in numbers played on her mind.

Almost before he could react, Jack was leaning over Zoe menacingly: Austin leapt to his feet, crossing the room in several strides, the expression on Zoe's face saying everything. He grabbed Jack's arm as he swung round and…

Yvette's scream seemed to break through Jack's subconscious.

"Aus, I'm so sorry!" He stepped forward, towards him.

"Get out of my house." Austin said quietly, through clenched teeth. "GET OUT!" He yelled when Jack didn't move.

Instinct kicked in as Jack left the house, slamming the door behind him, driving off at speed into the distance.

"Over here." Jack waved weakly, his heart pounding, his hands shaking.

Zoe looked as beautiful as ever, and she was his: he smiled with the thought. His smile disappeared: 'was' certainly described what they'd left behind. His heart wrenched at the thought that it was over. Almost certainly it was over, but… but there was a small chance.

He'd had, whatever the specialists had called it, some sort of stress associated breakdown. Jack never had been too clever with words. Zoe and Austin nodded, knowing what he meant. He knew they would, so he didn't worry about getting the technicalities right. Drawing a deep breath, he continued. He'd flipped his lid, they smiled at this metaphor, but that never excused his actions.

The news had reached him, in the rehab centre, that he'd hospitalised his best friend, and then everything fell into place. He'd lost not only his marbles, but his job, his wife and kids, and his friends.

"Hey, don't get me wrong," Austin cut in, "that was not a killer punch."

The three laughed, despite the awkwardness of the subject.

"Shock kicked in, and well, final straw for a hypo."

Jack winced. "Yes but if I hadn't been such an idiot, I wouldn't have hit anybody." His voice trailed off.

Zoe felt an overwhelming urge to get up and cuddle him. She bit her lip. Not for the first time, she wondered if moving their things from the house was the right thing to do.

Austin had helped her hire a company who went to the house, using her key, and collected the things she requested, transferring them to Cornwall. Most of what they'd retrieved belonged to Kim and Tom: Zoe felt that most of her belongings were tainted by the past.

It had been the same company that had moved Austin and Yvette to their Cornish residence when she had fallen so ill almost a year ago. Ironically, Zoe had helped him with their move - from the other side.

Reading Zoe's expression, Austin squeezed her hand, reminding her to be brave.

"Orange, anyone?" He broke the unwelcome silence,

getting to his feet.

His friends nodded, and with relief, he headed towards the bar. He'd known that there was something not right. Jack never went drinking; never mind coming home drunk. As for hitting anyone... Austin shook his head.

Why had they not seen there was something wrong? On second thoughts, he realised that he and Yvette being nowhere near their friends meant they couldn't have possibly known.

He had felt some apprehension when Jack had rang to say that he was coming down for a few days, and asked if he could see them - and perhaps the kids too - when they were all together? Since they'd last seen him, there had been numerous letters from Zoe's solicitor: not just about the sale of their house, Jack's health updates were frequent. With Jack's confession, and diagnosis, it was like all the pieces of the puzzle came together.

Over the last few months, Austin and Zoe had often stayed up late talking while the kids were asleep and Yvette too was safe in slumber. It would take time, and she'd never forget what had happened, perhaps she'd never truly forgive Jack, but she didn't press charges and didn't file for a divorce.

Turning round, laden with glasses, Austin's eyes fell on his friends, both looking into their laps.

"I'm sorry," he began, putting the drinks down, "I have to phone. I have to know Eve's still okay."

Both smiled at him, and were left alone again.

"How is Eve?" Jack asked.

Zoe looked up, and found herself staring right into his eyes. For a moment, she didn't recall what it was she was going to say.

She shrugged. "Much better than she was."

"Austin wouldn't have left her with Tom and Kim unless he felt sure she'd be alright."

Zoe took her gaze away from him. That was obvious, especially knowing Austin.

"I know what you're thinking," Jack continued.

Zoe looked up, confused and surprised at the same time, fearful of what he'd say.

"It's the drugs. I regained normality, apart from my weight." He patted his stomach. Jack had never been so big… well, he wasn't exactly big, about… she tried to judge …two sizes bigger? Then she realised she was eyeing him up, or this was what Jack would almost certainly think. She winced.

But Jack hadn't noticed – too busy cringing inside, convinced Zoe was thinking ill of him. It was a difficult fight against the weight, but he was determined. He'd never felt so scrutinised and self conscious.

Her eyes came back to him at the mention of her name.

"Zoe. D'you think…" he stopped, shaking his head.

"What?"

He still shook his head, taking a gulp of orange. "No matter."

"C'mon, what?"

"It's been so long. You look… beautiful." Tears welled in his eyes.

"Oh, Jack." She'd never seen him so emotional… except, of course, at the birth of Tom, and then Kim. Fatherhood overjoyed him: Zoe smiled at her memories. He seemed so fragile in comparison, now to then. She leant across the table, taking his hand in hers. "Hug?" She offered, trying to catch his eye.

Jack nodded, and they stood up, each clasping the other in close.

Grr… this was what she'd missed… Zoe squeezed her eyes closed as she squeezed him. Her husband. Her poor, unwell husband, who had gone through Hell without any of their help. For a moment, guilt swamped her – then common sense kicked in.

She had done exactly the right thing, of that there was no doubt. And in the same manner, taking him back was the right thing to do.

Austin stood to one side, watching and nodding to himself. He'd judged the situation right, so far. "Can I join in, or is this a private hug?" he asked.

They both laughed and arms parted to let him link up.

Chapter 7

Warily, Jack looked around. "Are you sure it's okay to be here?"

"Yes, of course." Austin beckoned him in, but Jack stopped where he was, a flashback unrolling. He jumped as Austin's hand touched his shoulder. "You okay?"

Jack shrugged, allowing himself to be led into the kitchen and sat down.

"We know about your illness and your medications, Jack. You lost control, but you're better now. Aren't you?"

"Yeah, I am. Just came over a bit funny there." He wiped at the sweat on his brow.

Austin frowned. "Funny? How?"

"Flashback. When I was last here," he half-laughed, "where I left and totalled the car on the way back."

"Totalled?" Austin repeated.

"That was when I realised there was something wrong: it took a bang on the head to bring me to my senses."

They lapsed into silence for several minutes before Jack found his voice again.

"I...I dunno if I can do this." His face was creased in anxious concern. "What do I say to the kids? How do I explain?"

"Don't worry about that, they know. They're already up to date."

"I've lost them. I've lost everything." Jack dissolved into tears.

"But you haven't, Jack."

Jack waved his comments aside.

"What happened wasn't your fault: it was out of your control. But we cannot turn back the clock, what happened,

happened. It takes time. You must work together as a family, because that's what you are." Austin paused, taking note that Jack's gaze raised from the floor. "You have wonderful kids and a fantastic wife. They understand. Jack, they might even forgive you, but you must be patient. Tom and Kim are the best kids, y'know. You and Zoe are great parents. The only thing you've lost is time. So make up for it."

Jack rubbed his head, feeling tired. "I'm not going to rush anything."

"Good." Austin smiled. "Coffee?"

Jack shook his head, and Austin frowned. "No can do. Caffeine causes an adverse reaction with me." He pulled a face. "Even decaf does me in. I'll just have water."

"Sure."

"Where is everybody?" Jack had listened while Austin was busy attending to hosting duties, but heard no signs of other life in the house.

"Have a look for yourself." Austin indicated out the kitchen window, half of his attention still on the task in hand.

Jack got up and walked around to look into the garden. At that exact moment, Zoe looked up. Seeing him, her face lit up and she headed towards the house. Jack walked away from the window, shaking.

"Are you sure you're..."

There was a dreadful thump as Jack hit the floor.

Zoe shrieked as she entered the house, seeing them both on the floor. Austin, kneeling beside him, had heaved Jack over onto his side, safe.

"It's okay Zoe, grab us that oil." Austin indicated the essential oil bottle on the windowsill. "Waft that under his nose, he's just passed out, I think."

Hastily she unscrewed the top of the mixture, following Austin's instructions. "Jack? Jack, can you hear us?" She paused, squeezing his hand and gently wafting. The aroma did the trick - Jack moaned.

"He came over funny a few minutes ago. But he didn't say he felt unwell." Austin explained.

Zoe nodded. "Can you sit up, d'you think?" She turned her attention to Jack. He was still shaking, she could feel and see. "I'm calling a doctor." Zoe got up from his side, reaching for her phone.

"No." Jack spoke firmly, gritting his teeth and sitting up. "I'm fine. I...I just need to lie down. I'm sorry." He was fighting back tears again as his head swam.

Austin nodded at Zoe, who left the room, then he turned to Jack. "Have some water and when you feel better, I'll help you stand up. Has this happened before?"

"Mmm..." he nodded, sipping the cool liquid, rubbing at his head again. "No."

"Headache?"

"Pressure." He allowed Austin to help him sit back up on the chair, once he'd reassured him that he wasn't going to pass out again. "You must do nothing but look after people." He joked, looking into his friend's concerned expression, glad when Austin smiled.

"I hate black outs, you lose all sense of where you are and what's going on." Austin was beginning to feel sorry for his friend.

Jack nodded in agreement. His heart was racing. "Please Aus, I want to lie down."

"When you feel able to walk, we'll go."

Jack nodded, and got to his feet shakily. They made slow progress along the corridor to what had become Zoe's room; she had gone ahead, and preparations were all made.

"So tired today."

"Didn't you sleep very well?"

Jack shook his head. "Too noisy, and the bed's... not comfy."
Zoe and Austin looked at each other and made a silent decision. It was obvious that Jack was not well.

"Our doctor will be in to see you tomorrow morning," Zoe began, "you're to stay in bed until then."

"You're staying here from now on." Austin continued. "I'll get your things and settle up."

Jack nodded, thanking him quietly.

"You okay here?" Austin asked her: it was Zoe's turn to nod. "I'll tell Eve, and be back soon."

"Jack?" She spoke softly, feeling his hot cheeks with the back of her hand.

But Jack was already asleep.

Chapter 8

"Hey Eve," Jack smiled, kissing her hand, making Yvette smile, "how're you?" He had sensed someone else in the room, someone other than Zoe.

"It makes a change to have someone else play invalid." She teased.

He laughed, rubbing sleep out of his eyes.

"I'm alright," she tapped the dressing table lightly, "touch wood. How're you feeling?"

Jack groaned, touching his head.

Yvette frowned. "Still sore?"

His heartbeat was calmer now. Lying here, he could smell Zoe: her scent filled his nose. As far as he was concerned, this was heaven.

"Hey," Zoe stuck her head round the door, "what're you doing in here?" She playfully scolded Yvette, her eyes falling on Jack, their hands intertwined. "I hope you're not disturbing him."

"As if I would, I know what it's like." Yvette spoke softly.

Kicking herself, Zoe drew nearer. "Oh Eve, I didn't mean it like that, babe." Immediately she came closer, cuddling her shoulders. "I'm sorry, I didn't mean to upset you."

Yvette shook her head, happy for Zoe's comfort.

Zoe caught Jack's eye. It was so good to have him back, and now they knew it was just a flu-virus: just, Zoe corrected herself, the poor soul had been up half the night with a raging fever. She had missed him, the hurt ran deeper than she'd let herself believe.

Yvette moved to pull away from their hug and Zoe let go of her. "I'll leave you two alone," she paused as Jack yawned, "assuming Jack doesn't fall asleep before I get out the room."

Zoe smiled at her tease, lying down on the bed beside Jack and cuddling into him. Jack was struggling to keep his eyes open, soon drifting into sleep. It was her scent, and warmth; it soothed him in a way he couldn't explain.

On a mission, Austin had the laptop out, Jack's medication beside him. He looked up, abandoning everything when he saw Yvette – seeing also that she was upset. His heart pounded as he wrapped her in his arms.

"Don't let me go, don't ever let me go." She whispered.

Austin almost pulled away in surprise. "What d'you mean?"

"I can't... I can't face life without you, Aus."

"Eve, I'm always here for you sweetheart, you know that. What brought this on?"

Yvette dissolved into tears, unable to speak, clasping him in tightly.

At that moment Zoe came back into the room, her coat in her arms. "Right, Jack's asleep, so I'm going for Tom and Kim... Eve, what's wrong?"

"What did you say to her?" Austin said quietly, anger in his voice.

Zoe looked up at his tone. She relayed what had happened, but that wouldn't have upset Yvette, surely not this much?

Austin shrugged, and Yvette moaned; his face paled: things suddenly all made sense. Without saying anything more, he headed for their bedroom, sweeping Yvette up into his arms while he sat with her in the middle of their bed. Zoe followed, confused, leaving her coat on the sofa behind her.

"You better go and pick the kids up." He said as Zoe hovered in the doorway.

"But what's happening?"

Yvette looked like she was asleep, but she was shaking, her whole body trembled.

"She's going to have a fit. Zoe, go. There's nothing we can do."

Zoe was shocked at how calmly Austin spoke; she came and sat on the edge of the bed. She was almost fascinated, never having experienced her friend's condition.

Yvette cried against him, shaking in his arms. Austin rocked her, trying to soothe her, knowing that there truly was nothing they could do, knowing it would pass. It had been a while since the last one, and this was a permanent reminder of what she had come through in the last year.

"Zoe, go." Austin repeated.

"Okay, if you're sure."

He nodded and Zoe left, but not before checking again on Jack.

As she drove the now familiar roads, her mind turned over and over. They couldn't stay with Yvette and Austin forever, they had to find their own place. It wasn't fair to over burden their friends; they must feel like they have no peace in their own home.

But could she look after Jack, and the kids? And hold down some sort of job to pay the bills? It was lovely down here by the coast. They'd never afford a house like Austin and Yvette's on the beachfront, but further in, perhaps...

Would Jack recover and find himself again? Would he terrorise them again if he relapsed? Zoe swallowed hard, she couldn't go through all that again.

Chapter 9

Jack moaned and Zoe cuddled into him. "Everything hurts..." He paused, launching into another sneezing fit. "That doesn't help."

"I know, Jack. You'll be alright in a few days." Zoe attempted to comfort him, combing her fingers through his short hair, carefully studying his face.

"Zoe,"

"Uh-huh,"

"I love you."

"Aww!" Zoe broke into a smile, kissing him and squeezing him tightly. "I love you too Jack, very much."

Just as she thought he'd fallen asleep, his voice broke the silence around them. "Zoe, what's happened to Yvette?" He opened his eyes to look at her.

"Nothing to worry about, Austin said there's nothing we can do." She paused as Jack's eyes widened. "She has these fits, every so often. Takes her time to recover, that's all. She'll be okay. Let's focus on getting you better."

Sorrowfully, he shook his head. "It's my fault."

"No, Jack. It just happens."

Jack shook his head, his expression betraying his thoughts. "I've made her ill." He groaned.

Zoe cuddled him tightly. "It's not your fault. Don't worry, Jack. We need you better first before we do anything to help Aus and Eve. You're tired, you need to sleep. Close your eyes. I'll soon be coming to bed as well."

Waiting until he was asleep again, she tiptoed out of the room so as not to disturb him. Spending time with Tom and Kim before they went to bed, she checked on her friends before going to bed herself. All in all, this took about two hours.

Fortunately, Austin had been right: Yvette had soon come around, and was starting to regain what passed for normality. The atmosphere in the house lightened considerably.

Coming quietly into the room, she did her best to not disturb him, but Jack's groan for her told her she hadn't been successful in this.

"Shh. It's okay, I'm here." Slipping into bed beside him, she pulled the duvet over her.

"Zoe, I'm sorry."

"What for?" She couldn't see his face, her eyes not yet adjusted to the darkness.

"I shouldn't have come down..."

"Why not?"

"I don't want to pass this onto everyone else. You've all been so nice, and forgiving. And understanding." He shook his head. "I almost can't believe it."

There was nothing Zoe could say to that.

"Zoe, I know you may, well you may not want to talk about it, but... I never meant to hurt you, you know that, don't you?"

"I know." She spoke so softly, Jack worried he'd upset her; he turned over, beckoning for a hug.

Zoe let him. She noticed that now he'd always asked her if it was okay to kiss her, or hug her, and he was so dubious of touching her. But there was always a memory there, in his hesitation, of how good it felt. She sensed this mixture of emotions in him.

"Are you okay? I mean, I know Austin's been looking after you all, but... I didn't cause you any... damage, did I?"

Zoe shook her head, squeezing him. "We should talk about

this, all of this, but not now Jack. You're ill and it's late. We need to sleep."

"Sorry, Zoe. Of course, and I don't want to hurt you by dragging up the past. Tell me if I go too far."

Silence lapsed between them.

"I know you've just politely told me to shut up, but I have to say one more thing. I don't expect you, or the kids, or anyone, to forgive or forget what happened. I've kept alive just thinking that there was a small chance that we might, one day, be a proper family again."

Zoe held her tongue. Squeezing her eyes shut, she recalled the conversation she'd had with Austin on this very subject, and not so long ago either. Tears slipped down her face.

"Zoe, you are my life. I have nothing to live for if I don't have you. I want to make love to you, so sweetly and passionately, to show you how much I love and want you. But it'll be a long time before we can break through the emotional barriers, before we'd be ready to be truly reunited."

Zoe was speechless. The old Jack would never be so sensitive. Shamefully, she found herself turned on!

"I had to tell you how I feel. It'll be an uphill struggle, a battle to get through the 'ghosts' and the horror, I know, but I'm not going to give up, not ever." He kissed Zoe's head, unaware that this action made her melt.

In her own mind, she'd had this conversation many many times: she knew she'd come to a decision. She felt his forehead - not burning tonight. He was dreadfully congested, and positively reeked of menthol rub. Mmm... but how good it felt to be in these strong arms. And he was cuddly, the extra weight was not a problem to her mind, she'd always thought that he was too thin and straggly anyway.

They fell asleep in each other's arms.

She woke, still with her head on Jack's shoulder, her arm draped across him. Smiling then, she recalled their late night conversation.

Her Jack had changed so much, whether it be due to his stress related illness or not, but it didn't matter, he was still hers and she loved him. They shouldn't alienate him because of what had happened... but it was such a delicate subject.

She began to stroke him automatically as she let her thoughts roam... smiling a different smile. Jack stirred.

"Were you having a naughty dream?" She teased.

"I was dreaming about you; about us."

"Oh yeah?" She began to caress him.

"What are you doing?" Jack moved to turn over, but Zoe stopped him. "Zoe, let go of me."

"You're such a sexy man, Jack. I desire you." She began to kiss him all over, exciting him more.

His heart was pounding, what was Zoe doing?! Surely this was wrong, wasn't it? He moaned as she kissed him all over. His manhood wasn't complaining, he could feel it grow and throb, but he felt so confused.

Only last night they'd... oh my God, Zoe scrambled on top of him, pinning him to the bed, easing herself down onto him. It had been so long... and the sex was so good...

His next movements were automatic: his fingers reached down to her clitorial hot spot, his other hand caressing her breasts. She moaned encouragingly. He rolled over, positions reversed, the feeling building. She climaxed several times: Jack holding out for as long as he could before letting the sweet release out, crying out her name.

They collapsed on top of each other, trying to get their breath back. It felt so good, Zoe didn't know if they should've done that, and Jack had similar thoughts, but it felt right. She recovered quickly, but he was left panting, gasping for air: Jack's head thumped as the adrenaline coursed through his veins.

Jack sat bolt upright, sweat trickling down his brow, causing Zoe also to jump awake. First, he was horrified and panic stricken, then confused. Reality filtered into his mind. It was a dream, thank goodness it was just a dream...

Then he caught Zoe smiling at him, and the realisation sunk in. That hot romp was real! He grimaced. But wait, Zoe didn't seem to mind... she was stroking him, talking to him.

"Sorry Zoe, what did you say?"

"I said, are you alright?"

Jack nodded, smiling, making her smile too.

"It certainly wasn't a dream Jack, you naughty man." She added. He wrapped his arms around her and she nuzzled against his shoulder. "Now that was good," she murmured, kissing him.

But the sinking feeling was still there. "I love you Zoe, so much."

"I love you too, Jack."

Allowing his hands to wander all over her body, he could feel the tears building up again, and tried to hold them back. "I've missed you so much, Zoe. I've dreamt of this." He whispered.

"I've missed you so much." She pulled away slightly, looking into his eyes. "I don't know if that happened at the right time, but it felt right." She smiled. "It always does with you."

He grinned. "Thank God I remember how," he whispered, making her laugh. "And thank God I have such a beautiful wife, even after all that's happened. I don't know what I've done to deserve you, Zoe."

Chapter 10

"Bloody Jack," Yvette murmured.

Austin gently soothed her, rubbing her chest. "C'mon Eve, you can't blame Jack, these things happen."

Influenza doesn't just happen, she wanted to reply, but she didn't have the strength. While it was true that the more people around, there were more germs, and with the kids here, more germs got through. But nothing had affected her this much.

Maybe it was because of the recent fit that she was more susceptible; or maybe not. Some viruses were more destructive than others, especially if you already had a weakened immune system, as she did.

Her head throbbed, but her chest was the worst. The pain and the horrid burning sensation. And the deep wrenching choking cough made even Austin wince. Every cold attacked her chest, being an asthmatic this was a common weakness.

"Will you be okay if I pick you up?" Austin knew how much this reassured her: carefully cradling her in his arms when she nodded.

The constant changing of her temperature did not help. Too hot one minute then shivering, then sweating. Her symptoms had worsened over the last few hours; he hoped that they would disappear as quickly as they'd come on; hoping also to avoid having to call in a doctor.

What also worried him was that the virus was highly contagious, and he dreaded to think what havoc it would play with him. Yvette was sobbing against him now, and he too was on the brink of tears, wishing.

Zoe shooed Tom and Kim from the bedroom doorway, coming to her friends' side quickly. Austin bit back his thoughts when she chuntered her apologies; shaking his head, mentally putting up the barricades. She got the message and left them alone, closing the door quietly behind her.

If ever there was the time that they needed to move out, this was it. It wasn't fair to burden them, first psychologically, then physically with the kids, and now Jack as well. They all needed out.

"What're you doing?" Jack came to her side, reading the adverts she'd frantically circled and crossed out, some of them she'd treated equally within the last hour.

They were still talking about it when Austin came into the room, a few decisions made.

"..." Jack stopped abruptly as Zoe kicked him. "Ow! What was that for?" He turned to her as they were left alone again. "Yvette's always ill..."

This time Jack broke off as Austin re-entered the room and grabbed hold of him, virtually lifting him out of the chair. The expression on his face frightened both Jack and Zoe.

"Yvette was fine until you arrived." Austin was shaking with rage, but within a few minutes, he released his grip on Jack. Turning to Zoe as he started to leave the room. "I have to get Eve to the hospital, she can't breathe properly."

Zoe and Jack gasped in horror.

Zoe jumped to her feet, grabbing her keys from the side. "I'll take you. You keep an eye on her, I'll drive."

"Isn't it easier to get an ambulance?" Jack too got to his feet.

Austin shook his head, continuing to head back to Yvette. Jack had followed Austin through and stood in their bedroom, horrified to see – and hear – what state Yvette was in.

Left feeling totally useless as he watched them disappear, and ever so guilty, Jack knew what Austin had said was true. He had infected her with his virus; this was his fault. He prayed that Yvette would be alright; that they'd all be alright.

"I...I couldn't do anything." Zoe whispered, tears flooding down her face, burying herself into his chest the minute she arrived back.

She was distraught; he felt a wreck himself. It was selfish he knew, but he couldn't get it out of his head that this was all his fault.

"What did they say?" He asked her gently.

By now, it was obvious that Austin would be staying with Yvette overnight.

Zoe shook her head and shrugged. "Where are Tom and Kimmy?"

"They're in bed, they went about half nine when you didn't come home."

She nodded, escaping from his clutches to sit down.

Jack automatically clicked on the kettle. "Tea?" She nodded again. "Zoe, you didn't eat, let me make you something."

She shook her head. "I can't, my stomach's in knots. I keep seeing it, they've linked her up to all these machines..." her voice trailed off.

As he went to speak, her phone went off: Zoe couldn't answer it fast enough.

"Austin?" Her heart was in her mouth. She could sense Jack behind her.

"They've got her stable." Austin tiredly rubbed his face. He looked and felt exhausted.

"Oh thank God!" Zoe breathed a relieved sigh, glad of Jack's arms around her. "I'll come in tomorrow, about ten."

Austin nodded. "Okay, see you then." The screen went blank, the call ended.

Jack had to remind himself not to take it personally that Austin hadn't said anything to him: his mind was on Yvette, nowhere else.

Yvette was safely in a drug-induced sleep, although she was wearing the oxygen mask. He caressed her flushed cheeks, holding her hand, simply watching her breathing. Eventually he too drifted off, but he only slept fitfully, too anxious to relax.

He wasn't the only one having problems sleeping. Jack felt like he needed the sleep to once and for all get rid of the residues of the virus, but his whirling mind did not allow it.

Zoe slept late as he packed the kids off to school and arranged some viewings with the local estate agent by the time she rose around 9.30 am.

Chapter 11

Yvette knew Austin was there; she could smell the faint trace of his aftershave. Then she registered his hand holding hers. Suddenly her heart beat shot up.

"Easy, Eve. It's okay." Austin heard footsteps coming across the hall to them. "You're alright sweetheart, I'm here."

"Nice deep breaths, that's it, nice and easy." Yvette was confused by the masculine deep voice alongside Austin's soft comforting tone. "The Doc's on his way. He's coming to you first, you lucky girl." He squeezed Austin's shoulder: it was Austin's turn to feel hesitant.

The grip on his hand tightened, mimicking the tightening of Yvette's chest. She gave a pained groan.

He squeezed her hand back. "Easy sweetheart, you're okay. It'll go away soon, try to relax."

Yvette wanted a hug but it was too sore. Could she get through to him what she needed...? No, the cure was also the blackness, and once she was in its grip, she couldn't do much to resist...

"Eve?" Austin was stroking her cheek again: she pulled back into consciousness. "Hang on sweetheart, the doctor's here."

She wept but soon stopped, the motion causing too much pain to bear. Next thing she knew there was a curious floating sensation, a feeling that had almost become normality.

When she next awoke, there were two people by her side.

"Hey Eve, I'm right here." Zoe spoke quietly, having been warned to keep her voice low.

Yvette clenched her teeth, remembering the pain. "Aus!" His name came out as a wail.

They were both speaking to her; soothing her: she had this as background, vaguely aware of Zoe stroking her hair as she tended to do, but also aware of the tension around her. Austin ever so carefully leant over her.

Yvette was too shattered to lift her arms to go around him, realising then that she couldn't move. Oh God no! Not the paralysis, please no, not the paralysis, please...

"Can you hear me, Yvette? Hang on, my love. The drugs are helping you. Don't fight anything, sweetheart. You need to rest."

Austin... Austin... Even in her mind Yvette sobbed, only able to say his name. His words were muzzy and confused, none of them properly getting through to her. Then, the pain struck. It was a stabbing pain, and it dragged her under.

The drugs wrestled it, controlling it: she fell asleep again, only to wake up hours later coughing. A deep, agonising, rasping cough that hurt beyond words.

She wheezed through Austin's comfort, wrapped in a drug-controlled mixture of comfort and pain. His words were hard to take onboard, more than hard; hard to decipher over the sound of her own awful, laboured breathing.

"Hi there gorgeous, how are we feeling today?"
She'd opened her eyes, and this was a mistake she knew: closing them again quickly. Who was this guy and why was he so bloody cheerful?! Yvette flinched.

"You're making steady progress, perhaps they'll let you home soon."
She moved her hand - her whole arm had life now, thank God - searching for Austin's hand.

"Your hubby's gone out for some fresh air but he'll be back soon."

Yvette opened her eyes wide.

"I've opened the window."

Trying to take a deep breath of the fresh air coming to her, she was aware that it felt good. Then she coughed and clutched her chest, and her stomach hurt too.

"All that coughing has left you very sore."

Yvette nodded.

"Your hubby's been very good, very devoted. Wish my man was like that." He pulled a face: Yvette tried to hide her bemused expression. "But enough about me. It's time for your test." Yvette's expression turned to horror. "It's nothing to worry about. I don't suppose you know how long you've been here?"

"Few days maybe." She shrugged.

He laughed. "You've been here a lot longer than that. It's been almost two weeks since your hubby came in with you cradled in his arms, but you wouldn't remember. You've been quite under the weather, but we've seen to that."

"Austin." She raised her arms, beckoning him for a hug as he entered the room. "I didn't know..."

"You were too far out of it." He smiled at Stuart, now quite used to the man's presence. "I'm so glad we got you here in time. My poor darling, you've been so ill."

In time?! Horror cascaded over her.

Stuart returned his smile. "I'll leave you to it, if there's anything you want, just ring."

Austin nodded, thanking him; holding Yvette tighter, realising she was shaking now, imagining the horrid thoughts in her head. His words of reassurance came out automatically: and this time she was able to respond to his declaration of love.

"Careful, I'm… still delicate," she warned as Zoe hugged her. It's good to be home, she allowed herself to think.

"It's good to be home, isn't it Eve?"

She smiled as Zoe spoke the thought in her head, resting against Austin's shoulder, aware she was the centre of attention. "Sure is." She closed her eyes, concentrating on her breathing.

Listening to Austin's quiet soothing, she was soon feeling sleep take hold of her once more.

"Mum, is Auntie Eve okay?" Yvette could just about make out Kim's voice.

"She's a lot better than she was, but she still needs to rest." Zoe replied.

Too right… Yvette silently agreed.

Kim nodded. "Will she be okay when we move?"

Move? Alarm bells rang in Yvette's head.

"I don't know, Kim. She might be, we'll have to wait and see. Off you go, I'll be through in a minute to see how you're getting on with your homework." Zoe turned back to them, seeing Yvette was wide awake. "We move next week." She beamed at her.

"Move?" Yvette repeated.

"We need our own space, and we cannot encroach on you two any more."

"Move?" Yvette repeated again, unable to take the news in. She nodded, aware that Zoe had been talking, presumably about the house and had stopped.

"Don't worry about it Eve, you need to rest still. I'm sure Aus will fill you in when you're feeling a bit better."

"In a few days, maybe." Austin nodded.

"Maybe." Zoe agreed. "Now rest, we'll give you peace. You'll be asleep in no time." She hugged her again, gently, before leaving them alone as promised.

Trying to think, Yvette frowned. "Austin..."

"Sshh. Plenty of time for questions Eve, but right now, you need to sleep. Zoe's right, you'll be out for the count any minute." He kissed the top of her head. "Rest, sweetheart."

It was almost as if Austin had read her mind, barely before she'd had time to think the thought, he began to soothingly rock her in his arms. For Yvette, this was the best feeling in the world. In her world.

Chapter 12

Time was a magical thing.

Months down the line, Jack had a job as a bank clerk, albeit an over-qualified one. He was happy enough, especially as there was no stress involved: the last thing he wanted was to chance any sort of relapse.

There were still times, he could sense, there was something that held them back, but communications were flowing freely. He swallowed all the apologies he kept wanting to let out, conscious of Zoe's wish not to be reminded of the horrors of the past.

But this was one of those times Zoe wouldn't say anything. She seemed to have terrible mood swings lately: one minute fine, then snap his head off in a flash. At times he felt like he was treading on thin ice! It reminded him of a saying that one of the younger clerks had coined: don't get all up in my grill, man. He had chuckled then, and chuckled now with the thought.

This lunchtime, she had left a tearful message on his phone, having come home unwell from her part-time job at the school. He tried calling her back, but the phone was off the hook.

Typical!

"Zoe?" The place was still a state, half decorated but tidy, he clomped through the bare boarded hallway. "Hello? Where is everyone?"

"Dad." Tom's voice floating along the corridors, directing him.

Jack's heart pounded. Please, please may she be okay...

He followed the voice through to the master bedroom, where Tom and Kim were both with Zoe.

"She's been sick." Kim pulled a face.

"She said she feels awful." Tom added as Jack sat on the edge of the bed where they were beside Zoe.

He could feel her hot forehead through his shirt as he cuddled her. "My poor Zoe," he told her quietly.

Tom continued. "I brought one of these, Mum uses them when we're not well."

Jack smiled, taking the cool patch from his son, placing it carefully across Zoe's burning forehead. Noticing the glass of water too that had arrived by the bedside, he knew that their offspring had done well looking after her.

"You'll have to do dinner." Zoe said weakly, keeping her eyes closed.

"That's okay, don't worry. Burnt sausages all round." He replied, making them all smile. "You two go'n turn the TV on, I'll make a start on dinner in a minute."

They left slowly, unsure.

"My poor Zoe, when did this come on?"

Zoe shrugged. "Loadsa viruses going round the school, little beggars give us their germs all the time. It's probably... just a... 48 hour thing." She winced as her head throbbed mightily.

Jack frowned, concern written all over his face. "I hope so. If you're not better by the morning, I'm phoning the doctor."

Zoe nodded, slowly, the throbbing in her head worse with movement.

"Have you eaten?"

She shook her head. "Couldn't." She whispered.

"You've gotta have something. I'll do you some soup, or whatever you want Zoe."

"Do yours first, I'm... gonna sleep."

"Okay. I'll come back and check on you every so often." He kissed her, watching her face for a while. She seemed okay, very pale and tired, but alright. "You sleep. I love you." Zoe smiled faintly. "I love you too, Jack." She whispered.

He had expected her to fight back as usual, and her lack of fight told him all he needed to know: Zoe was not well at all. She'd pulled herself to sit up against the pillows, and had managed to at least eat something the next morning.

Jack was torn, unsure of leaving her and going to work; if he wasn't so new, he'd phone in...

"I'll be fine." Zoe waved him out.

"Are you sure?" She nodded. "Okay, but I'll phone at lunch, and I'll try to leave a bit earlier."

There was no need but Zoe just nodded, it was much easier than trying to argue. He kissed her as usual before he left.

It was fortunate that the kids were, well, they weren't kids any more; they were teenagers now, Tom almost 16 and Kim 13. Tom had always looked after his little sister, even from an early age. Zoe smiled to herself, they were great kids.

She was thankful that Jack had pulled the fan towards her; it was turning into a fantastic summer, albeit a bit too warm at times. The heat made her feel sick, but she was aware that she'd better pull herself together and get up.

Zoe was combing her fingers through Yvette's hair, telling Yvette without words that she was there. They were alone for a few minutes while Austin was out of the room making tea, but she wasn't worried by the fact.

Returning to them after not that long, Austin was beyond relieved nothing had happened in his absence.

"Zoe..." Yvette moaned.

"Sshhh, it's okay Eve, I'm here. Austin's here too."

"It's twins…"

Zoe and Austin looked at each other. "What did you say, Eve?" Zoe asked her, still stroking her hair.

"You're… twins…" she murmured, making Zoe jump as she suddenly squeezed her hand. "…be careful…"

As Yvette fell asleep once more, Austin explained how Yvette had depressed herself, and him, thinking how wonderful Tom and Kim were, and what great parents they would've been. Though she hadn't let the extent of her feelings through, this was what had likely triggered her "drifting".

It'd happened before, and after a check up, Austin had put his worries to one side, knowing it was a matter of time until she recovered. She wasn't in any danger, he made sure of that in the first instance, so he was safe to keep a watch over her at home. It was similar to her having a fit; rest and TLC would do the job of restoring her strength.

Despite the explanation, Yvette's words still trickled through her mind. By lunchtime the next day, Zoe had driven herself daft, deciding to make a purchase to put her mind at rest. After all, there was a chance…

It'd been so long since she had done one of these home pregnancy kits: only she wasn't at home. She felt almost ashamed, locked in a public cubicle, listening to the footsteps of passersby and the running water.

One minute she couldn't, she waited but she couldn't pee; then it came in a surge and she dreaded that she'd engulfed the little stick, and that it wouldn't work; or worse, it would show the wrong result.

Paying with shakes, fumbling with wrappers
Walking on a thin blue line, waiting on a thin blue line…

It had been ages, simply ages, since her song writing. She was so focused on the task the words floated into her mind. Her eyes closed, willing the minute on. It seemed like an eternity; had it been this long when she'd done the others, years ago?

Did she want a positive result? Or a negative?

It was negative. Reality hit her with a jolt. She'd bought a twin kit... twin, the word haunted her. But, it was negative so there was no point really in trying another.

Disappointment flooded through her as she realised she'd been willing on that thin blue line. Her first reaction was of want: she wanted Jack to hug her and tell her it was alright. She shook herself, wiping at the tears that had slipped down her face.

She couldn't tell him. But then, she couldn't not tell him.

Chapter 13

"Jack..." Zoe's voice sounded softly in the other room.

"Uh-huh," he was rooted to the spot, fascinated by the programme, paint brush hovering in his hand. "Zoe?"

No reply.

Sighing, he put the brush down and walked across the room into the kitchen, the location of her voice. For a panicky minute he couldn't find his voice.

That moment, Zoe pulled herself to sit up. "Felt faint," she murmured.

Jack crouched on the floor by her feet, his arm around her, steadying her. "You're not gonna go, are you?"

Zoe shrugged, sitting hugging her knees, waiting for the feeling to subside. Jack rubbed her back gently, concern written all over his face.

"What's wrong?" Tom stopped in the doorway.

"I think it's just paint fumes making your Mum feel ill."

"Oh." He didn't know what to do now, already halfway out the door. "Is everything okay for me to go?"

Jack nodded. "Make sure you're back for dinner at six though, okay? And grab Kim when you're coming home."

"Okay."

They both winced as the door shut loudly behind him.

"I'm gonna lie down." Zoe got to her feet, surprised by how shaky she was.

Jack sprang to his feet, helping her to regain her balance. He insisted on making her comfy on the sofa so that he could keep an eye on her, swinging the windows open even wider.

Reassured she would be alright, he continued, aware that

the hall had been half-finished for too long. Painting was best done when there was peace, though he had to admit that Tom and Kim were very good at helping out, and didn't need to be asked twice.

They were super kids, he smiled to himself. He'd counted his lucky stars that his family had accepted him back so soon.

His whole life had changed: now it revolved around their growing needs, not his. There were times when he came out with things the old Jack would have never even thought about, and Zoe was taken aback. He knew he'd changed, and it was for the best.

Zoe growled to herself, annoyed that she felt unwell again. Serve her right for thinking the job would be easy - the admin office at the high school was normally quiet, but since the new term had started, work experience was fast approaching for the senior years. Between that, the phones constantly ringing, and the kids constantly interrupting - and some of them had no manners at all! - it was beyond hectic.

All the extra pressure had built up, no doubt contributing to her lower than usual immune system. Once she could get a hold of herself, she would continue to help Jack, determined to get the biggest of jobs in the house done first.

"It's okay Zoe, you're okay." Jack squeezed her hand, stroking her hair and face with his other hand. Now she was awake, he couldn't contain the grin any longer. "Do you remember, I don't suppose you do."

Her hand throbbed, as did her head; as she looked to find out why it hurt, she realised something wasn't right. Tears welled in her eyes. What the hell was going on? Why was she in the hospital, and why couldn't she remember anything?

Jack saw her confusion and set about reassuring her. "Don't worry Zoe, you're okay. As you fainted, you hit your head." Even he winced. "You'll be alright, I made sure of it." Leaning over, he cuddled her. "Zoe, I...I don't know how to tell you this." He smiled. "Normally it's the other way around."

Zoe looked at him, even more confused. Why did it hurt so much? Argh, and why did she still feel sick and dizzy?

"You're a coupla weeks gone. Well, more than a coupla weeks, and the baby's okay even after your fall." Zoe turned a paler as tears ran down her face. "But... the test was negative."

"I know, but these things can be wrong sometimes." Jack couldn't stop grinning. Six months ago it had looked like it was curtains for them, but now, what a difference. He could feel himself filling up.

"I got them to do an early scan. Look." Their first scan was in his hand. He squeezed Zoe, kissing her head. "I'm sorry you can't have any painkillers."

She smiled, silently thanking any and every God.

"You're to be checked over again before we can go home. I'm not letting anything happen to you, Zoe."

Zoe truly melted, squeezing him tightly. It was a miracle.

Chapter 14

Kim was aghast.

"Your parents must do it." Louise continued. "Your Mum's preggers, isn't she?"

"Yes ...ugh. That's disgusting!" Kim couldn't imagine it: well she could, but she didn't want to.

"Wonder what it feels like?" Beth spoke her thoughts aloud.

"What, sex? Or being pregnant?" Louise asked.

"Both."

"Sex is great." Louise grinned. "Don't worry, you two will soon catch us all up."

Beth looked across at Kim, and rolled her eyes.

"Hey, Stevie!" Louise yelled at a group of boys as they strolled by, obviously trying to impress the girls. She left to join them.

Beth rolled her eyes. "She's so fake, it makes me sick."

"D'you think?" Kim was impressed and it set her mind wandering.

"Oh, come on! She's not even fourteen; you're older than her. Anyway, who'd go out with her, never mind sleep with her!"

Beth seemed full of common sense, and Kim was glad to have her as a friend, but she admired Louise: she was so bubbly and self assured. Kim got tongue tied when any boy was around, but especially when she was around the one she liked.

He was quiet and studious, and she thought her parents would approve. Not that she'd ever have the courage to ask him out, because there was one problem - he was Beth's brother.

"You don't believe her, do you?" Beth's disapproving tone cut through Kim's thoughts.

"No, well, you've gotta wonder though."

Beth snorted. "She's all talk. And don't let her wind you up either."

Kim's mind skipped back to the Sex Education book they'd received. The pictures weren't that great, but from them it was easy to match the descriptions and it all looked like fun. But she'd had so many lectures about unsafe sex and being responsible, it rather killed the excitement.

She didn't want to get pregnant; she wanted to go to college with Beth, that was their plan. They would do the same course and flat share. It would be wicked to have their own place. Oh, but she'd miss her parents, and Tom.

He was an excellent big brother, the best. She knew he'd keep her secrets safe, and he always gave her sound advice. She wondered if he and his girlfriend Bryony were "doing it" - they were old enough. But she could never ask him!

They began to walk to their next class. It didn't help that she was one of the youngest in their year. Everyone else seemed more grown up and no-one seemed interested in her.

Yvette's words rang true. From the first scan it was hard to tell, but as Zoe's pregnancy progressed, the truth was revealed. How had she known?

Not that it mattered: Zoe was happy and Jack couldn't lose the grin from his face. This pregnancy was different to her others; she was more emotional and her mood swings came without warnings!

Through it all, Jack went with the flow. He displayed true qualities of unselfishness, pampering her every whim. Her colleagues, all female, were fantastically supportive, and constantly fussed around her.

That evening, Zoe went to bed ahead of him, telling him to wait for a few minutes before following her. His eyebrows raised in suspicion. There was a plan...

"Jack," she called to him softly.

He smiled to himself, coming into their bedroom, and closing the door behind him, seeing the light was on low, and she was ready for him.

"Come here, you sexy man."

"I don't need to be asked twice." He teased, slipping into bed beside her. Cuddling into her meant navigating the ever-increasing bump. She was giving him that look: Jack throbbed in delight. "My beautiful Zoe."

He kissed her, first her head, then her face and down her neck, making his way steadily down to kiss all of her body. Lying this close, he could feel the odd kick. The sensation awoke emotions inside of him he couldn't begin to describe.

"Don't stop," she whispered, "pleasure me, you naughty man,"

Jack was taken aback. Recently, she'd found sex uncomfortable. "Are you sure?" He kissed her again.

She tickled his bare body with her finger tips. "Let's see how it feels."

Jack couldn't believe how quickly she slipped on top of him: a movement an Olympic gymnast would be proud of. He supported her, his hands on her hips as she began to move slowly up and down.

Almost immediately he wanted to climax but managed to keep his control, Zoe recognised the signs and squeezed on him. It was so sensual; she'd heard that sex during pregnancy brought love making to another level for some couples, and certainly she could confirm this was true.

A long, low moan escaped from her throat as she increased the tempo. The only problem was she soon got out of breath and it seemed to take a long time to recover, making the sex intense.

She soon fell asleep, her arms locked around Jack, a smile on her face.

Chapter 15

"It would do us good to have a break, and Paris would tie in with our anniversary." Austin suggested.

Has it really been fifteen years? Yvette realised that she'd lost a fair chunk of that time. But throughout it all, Austin had been at her side. She didn't want to go, but she bit back the thought.

"What's wrong, Eve?" Austin caught her hesitation.

"I'm just not sure. How would we get there?"

"We'll drive. I know public transport's not an opinion, not even First Class all the way." He could see she was being swayed. "It'll be fantastic with the camera."

Yvette's love of photography had made a slow start, and Paris was just the creative boost she needed.

"What if I'm ill while we're away?" She said quietly, letting her gaze fall into her lap so as to avoid seeing his disappointment.

"Then we'll come home." Austin's reply was swift, as if he didn't need to think about it. In truth, he didn't.

Yvette shook her head sadly. "You can't look after me and drive. I'm such a burden, I'm sorry Aus."

"Yvette." Austin spoke so sternly, she looked up in surprise. "Don't think like that."

Tears slipped down her face: she roughly rubbed them away.

Taking hold of her hands, he kissed her. "You're not a burden, sweetheart. It's not your fault all the nasty things happened to you. I wish I could have the pain instead."

She was horrified at that idea. "Austin, no!" She squeezed him so tightly he gasped. "Don't say that. I...I can't live without you."

"I'm sorry Eve, I didn't mean to upset you. I just wish that I could take away your pain."

Yvette nodded, realising then that both of them were in tears.

Their door monitor warned of the presence of their friends, Austin took it as his cue to pull himself together. It was unusual for him to let Yvette see this side of his emotions. He got up then to meet them.

"We'll go." Her voice made him turn in the doorway back to her.

"Only if you're sure, Eve."

She nodded, smiling at him. "You're right, it will be nice to have a change of scene."

Austin nodded and smiled, closing the door over behind him. Closing her eyes once more, Yvette listened for the footsteps and voices.

It would do them both the power of good, and inject freshness into their photography. She knew Austin was right, if only she could get past the demons in her mind that told her otherwise...

"Eve?" Zoe stuck her head round the door.

Yvette opened her eyes.

"You okay?"

"Yeah,"

"You seem tired." She sat down on the bed, sweeping the fringe out of her eyes and running her fingers through her hair.

Yvette sighed, wrapped in her friend's arms. "You're getting bigger."

"I know, I feel as big as a bloody house." Zoe joked, relieved to see Yvette smile.

"I had a strange dream the other night. About you."

"Oh yeah?"

"You had triplets, two girls and a boy. Jack bought this enormous car, drove you home with the triplets in their car seats in the middle row of seats just behind the driver, with Tom and Kim behind them, almost sitting in the boot." She smiled at Zoe's bemused expression. "What?"

"We bought one of those. It's coming on Friday." Zoe paused as Yvette gasped in surprise. "I can deal with twins, but triplets?!" Zoe pulled a face.

Both of them laughed. What a handful!

"You'll be fine, you're a wonderful Mum – you are both wonderful parents."

There it was again, that hint of sadness in her voice. Zoe bit her lip, knowing she had something Yvette could only dream of. They needed a change of subject.

"I suppose Austin told you about Paris?" Yvette provided her own distraction.

Zoe nodded, enthused. "It sounds fabulous. Wish we could go; the most romantic city in the world!"

Yvette smiled faintly, and Zoe read her mind.

"You don't want to go, do you?"

Yvette sighed. "I do, but I'm frightened of being ill and ruining the trip."

"Oh Eve!" She cuddled her friend again. "You'll be alright. Austin'll look after you, even if something does happen."

"I know."

"Nothing will happen, think positive. You can't live your life in fear."

Yvette's subconscious spoke: I do anyway. It's not easy. Everything's happened to me. Me, all the time. And poor Austin always has to pick up the pieces. He has no life of his own.

Her thoughts were interrupted as Zoe grimaced. She'd

felt it too. One of the babies was active - it was hard to tell which one - but someone in there was having a good time.

"Zoe, are you okay?"

She pulled away from Yvette, rubbing her swollen stomach. "It's okay, don't worry Eve, quite normal. Probably two budding footballers in here, that's all."

Yvette smiled, unable to hide her relief, especially when Jack came through.

"Hey Eve,"

She smiled as Jack took her hand and kissed it.

"You look tired."

Hadn't she heard that before, somewhere? "At least I haven't got two budding footballers, as Zoe puts it."

"Aww, more movement?" Jack sat beside Zoe, rubbing her bump. "Listen to your Daddy, calm down in there."

They all laughed. However, Jack's voice did the trick.

"Still got it." He added, winking at Yvette. "C'mon Zoe, you've worn Eve out. We better give you peace. Tom and Kim'll be home soon looking for their dinner."

Yvette nodded, closing her eyes again. It was such a strange sensation: strange, but at the same time, nice. A physical link to the child you're carrying.

Something else she'd never experience. Her self hatred multiplied.

Austin came back into the room after seeing their friends out. Yvette feigned sleep, expecting him to leave once he knew she was alright. But he didn't. He stayed a while; first kissing her head and her cheeks, then her lips. She could feel his fingers over so softly stroking her face.

"I love you my Yvette, you're all mine. We'll always be together and I'll always look after you. Nothing you want or need is too much."

Tears spilled down her face then: she lifted her arms,

beckoning him in close. He felt so good to hold: likewise, it felt so good to be safe and warm in his arms; protected.

"I thought you were asleep," he whispered.

"I almost was," she said truthfully. "D'you always say that?"

"More or less. I want you to know that there's nothing for you to worry about. I often speak to you while you're sleeping, because you can still hear what I say, even though you're far away."

"Oh Aus, you are so sweet." More tears cascaded down her face. "I love you too, with all my heart."

Austin beamed, and began to kiss at her tears, soothing her.

"Oh Aus, you do all the right things."

"I do try." Ever so gently, he lifted her into his lap. "Now, time for a doze." He began rocking her. "While you sleep, I'll pack."

"Pack?" Yvette opened her eyes. "We're going now?"

Austin laughed. "Not now, but in the morning. We may as well, there's nothing holding us back. Jack and I arranged it as you and Zoe had your chat. I even called Ian and ran a few ideas by him."

Ian, their publisher, was fanatical about France - so much so, he'd given Austin a few ideas and locations. Yvette fell asleep with a smile on her face. Here he'd arranged the trip in no time and they were off. That was the beauty of having no ties: the world was their oyster.

Austin's voice disturbed her the next morning, long before she wanted to get up. She groaned her protest.

"Eve, I want to get going. You can sleep in the car."

Only half awake, she murmured in agreement: soon swept out to the car.

Zoe and Jack were house-sitting, and the car was already packed. It hadn't taken long because they didn't need much.

It was a week-long trip, at the most. Yvette agreed and just prayed she'd be alright.

"I've got a blanket if you want one." He offered.

Yvette shook her head, snuggling instead into one of his jumpers. She fell asleep easily, wrapped in the security of his scent.

The journey across the Channel was amazing, they drove onto the train in a line of cars and got out, locked up and settled down. It was quite an engineering feat to have a tunnel built from one country to another under the sea.

Soon reaching their destination, and in the rain, Austin remained optimistic; there was a good weather forecast ahead. He ran the proposed schedule by her, and of course Yvette agreed. He always covered everything they wanted and thought to include anything that may interest her.

Chapter 16

Austin frowned into his phone, confused by the tearstained expression greeting him. "Zoe, what's wrong?"

"Bring her back!" Zoe was in floods of tears, her voice high and panicky.

"What are you talking about?" Austin was becoming more confused by the second.

"Yvette... she's dying..." Zoe sobbed.

Austin could see Jack had arrived in the room now and tried to calm her down: he was thankful for his intervention.

"What's going on, Aus?" Jack asked.

"I don't know. You tell me."

"There's a news report saying Yvette's dying after a bad asthma attack..." Jack stopped as he read his friend's expression, realising there was perhaps a bend in the truth here. "Are you both okay?"

"We're fine. It's very hot and humid here and Eve had a minor attack. I took her to the hospital to be on the safe side. They gave her a breathing treatment on the nebuliser and she's fine." He paused. "Where did you hear this?"

"On the local news."

"How the hell did they know about that?!" Austin could feel his anger rising.

Jack shrugged, facing the screen he cuddled Zoe, soothing her.

"I'll sue when I find out! They have no right to intrude on our privacy!" Austin seethed.

There was a moment of silence.

"Didn't you say Eve's a big name over there?" The thought suddenly came to Jack.

"Well, there have been French translations. But I don't see what that's got to do with it."

Zoe sniffed. "I'm sorry, Aus."

"Don't worry, Zoe." Austin softened, getting her to look back into the screen. "Eve's okay, I promise. I wouldn't let anything happen to her."

"I know."

"Good. Now go and have a lie down. It won't do you any good getting all wound up."

Zoe nodded and Jack smiled.

"I'll phone when we're back, should be sometime Friday evening." Austin reminded them, before they exchanged goodbyes.

Austin sat in a moment of silence, shaking his head. Then he returned to Yvette, who he'd left in bed in the next room while he took the call.

"How're you feeling, sweetheart?"

"I'm okay." She whispered.

Austin smiled. "That's good. Zoe and Jack are alright, they were checking up on us."

Yvette nodded, receiving a brief half-hug; Austin didn't want to squeeze her while she was feeling delicate. She fell asleep smiling, reviewing the places they'd been and the photographs they'd taken along the way.

It came to light that the hotel was to blame. Cameras had been installed for security reasons and as Yvette's illness registered, an alarm tripped, and one thing led to another. Once the paparazzi got hold of it, well, any story of "famous" visitors was immediately escalated, with all sorts of incidents blown totally out of proportion.

Yvette had been deeply affected by this, despite Austin's best efforts. He worried what it would do to her, desperately hoping that it wouldn't trigger a downfall.

Beth's room was huge compared to hers - Kim couldn't fail to be impressed. It was strange to think of spending the night at someone else's house, which she'd done once before, only that didn't count.

She gave a little shudder. That was ages ago, when she and Tom were moved down here to stay with her Mum, and Austin and Yvette.

"You okay?" Beth asked her.

"Yeah,"

"You can have the bed, and I'll take the air bed."

Kim was horrified. "No, the airbed will do me. Just don't get up in the middle of the night and stand on me!"

Beth laughed. "Drink?" She reached for the bottle, unscrewing it carefully.

"What on earth is that?" The liquid was dark like Coke but it didn't smell like Coke.

"It's D&B - dandelion and burdock."

Kim pulled a face.

"Try it, it's really nice." Beth poured out a glass full for each of them, encouraging her to sip. Despite her initial thoughts, Kim had to agree, it was an unusual taste but she quite liked it. "Mixed with vodka it's great." Beth continued.

"Oh no." Kim covered her glass. "No thanks."

"Go on, one won't do you any harm." Beth tried to tempt her. "I've got Breezers for later - you'll have them, won't you?"

"I'm okay with them, but vodka makes me sick." Kim's cheeks reddened with the admission.

Beth realised that her friend was embarrassed by the truth in this. "Okay, I won't force you."

She dropped a bit into her own glass, Kim noticed.

Silently praising herself for saying no and staying firm, not that she ever thought Beth would force her into doing something she didn't want to.

"Ever done tarot before?" Beth pulled a deck of cards from one of her unit drawers.

Shaking her head, Kim eyed the cards suspiciously; they didn't look like normal playing cards.

Beth gave her a briefing and placed some "instructions" by her, explaining that she was learning and that this was what she was going to do on the side at college to make a bit of money.

She gave a run down of which cards meant what, and began, asking Kim to firstly pick three cards. Kim smiled, she was sure her friend was making this up, and by glancing at the sheet of Beth's handwritten scrawls, she could see there was a lot of leeway between what you could tell someone. It seemed harmless fun.

Beth promised that she'd teach her too: saying that in her future, she would marry a handsome young man, have a gorgeous big house on top of a hill overlooking the sea and would pass her exams with flying colours.

They cracked open the Breezers and turned up the music; after a few drinks, Kim was shocked by the things her friend came out with.

This was great, just the two of them, relaxed and in peace. She could feel the alcohol taking effect and hoped that it wouldn't make her ill, as happened with vodka. It only made her light headed and relaxed – so far.

"C'mon Beth! You must like someone, there's loadsa guys in our year."

Coming over solemn, Beth nodded. "Promise you won't tell anyone?"

"It won't leave this room." Kim swore. She shrieked with

laughter when her friend told her. The expression on Beth's face made her contain the rest of her laughing fit, while she explained her thoughts. "I had you pegged for Paul, or Gary."

Beth tilted her head to one side, a quizzical look on her face. "Why?" But she nodded along with Kim's reasoning. "C'mon, your turn."

"No, I don't fancy anyone."

"You must like someone!"

"Well..." Kim blushed. "I dunno if I can tell you."

"Go on. You know it won't leave this room."

"Promise?"

Beth nodded. "Promise."

"And you won't go mad?"

"Why would I go mad?" Beth took a long slug of her drink. "Nothing you can say will shock me."

She sprayed the mouthful of liquid when Kim whispered the name; Kim laughed despite her fear of her friend's reaction, banging Beth on the back as she coughed and choked.

"Well, I don't know if I fancy him. I mean, he's nice, and I like him. But we're all good friends, I wouldn't want to ruin that friendship. Or ours." Kim continued.

Beth nodded, having recovered from her coughing fit.

"Thought you said I wouldn't shock you?" Kim teased.

"I didn't know you were going to say my brother!" Beth retaliated.

Chapter 17

It was turning into a roaring hot summer, much to Zoe's distaste. With Jack at work and the kids at school, she spent a lot of time with Austin and Yvette, not wishing to be alone.

Jack was jealous he was not the one Zoe spent time with. This of course, couldn't be helped, and seemed silly, but he could not deny the way he felt. Underlying this, he knew, was fear: a fear for Zoe, and a fear that he would miss something. What if's crowded his mind, but there was nothing he could do.

Zoe had spent more time at home than at work since the discovery. The age of thirty four wasn't considered almost too late, or even too old, however the carrying of twins was unique "later in life", hence she was under the care of a specialist consultant this time around.

Fortunately, it was a smooth pregnancy, with not many of the associated ailments and minor morning sickness. She was more tuned in to emotions; and not just her own: Yvette helped her and always delighted in feeling a movement or a kick, but Austin strangely kept his distance.

He said it wasn't his place, but Zoe knew this was a charade that hid his personal pain. Even when she hugged him, Austin was ever so gentle, not that he wasn't anyway, and backed off quickly. She couldn't find the right words to break down these barriers.

He fought with himself not to immediately get up when Zoe sat down beside him. In truth, he didn't let himself dwell on the matter, knowing it would cost him his self-control. Jealousy burned within him: his friends didn't know how lucky they really were to lead normal and perfect lives.

Sometimes he couldn't help but yearn - but Yvette always was his number one.

All of these emotions he put to the back of his mind. These sort of thoughts triggered Yvette's meltdowns, and it always fell to him to be on top of things - and to be strong enough to stay on top.

Zoe stretched out, touching his arm to get his attention from his thoughts. Austin jumped, shaking off her smile of apology. "Aus, are you okay? You look so... sad. And far away." She rubbed his arm, and for a minute, his reaction to pull away slowed.

Austin visibly winced, and Zoe frowned. Could she read his mind? "I'm fine." He sighed. "I'm going for a walk. I'll tell Eve."

"Should I come with you?"

Austin shook his head. "Stay with Eve, please." Zoe nodded. "I'll see you later." Then, he was gone.

Zoe jolted out of her thoughts as Yvette spoke, coming into the room, several minutes later.

"What's going on?"

"What d'you mean, Eve?"

"Why's he gone?" Yvette seemed confused and a bit frightened.

"Sometimes he needs a bit of P&Q, I guess." She shrugged. "Whatever it is, he'll sort it out and come back and tell us."

Yvette's fallen face spoke volumes.

"C'mere you." Zoe gave her a hug. "Try not to worry. Jack does this every so often; he goes into his own little world for a while. Normally when he's thinking about something and wants peace to work it all out."

Yvette nodded, but she still felt upset; like it was something she'd done. There and then, she decided to leave him a message, in case he needed a little sign.

How nice it was sitting here, not a soul around him, no noise but the birds calling and the sound of the sea. Those magical sounds: the waves crashing and the gentle lulling of water lapping the shore.

The phone began to dance, the ringer on vibrate, Austin smiled to himself as he reached for it. He frowned seeing the sender information and almost rushed to his feet before he'd read it. Stopping, he opened it, a broad smile breaking across his face. His Yvette really was something else.

Kim was eagerly anticipating the night, awaiting her lift to Beth's party. Before she disappeared, Jack was determined that he was doing the right thing letting her go out.

"Got enough money?"

"Yes Dad, plenty of money." Kim replied patiently.

"And your phone, so you can call me to pick you up?"

"Yes Dad,"

"You will phone me, won't you, when you're finished?"

Kim sighed. "Yes Dad."

"Take a jacket with you, it'll be cold out tonight when you're finished."

Kim rolled her eyes. When Tom laughed, Kim shot him daggers. Relieved when Beth's Mum's car pulled up, she saw her escape. "I'm off," she scooped up her denim jacket on her way out the door.

"Be careful and have fun. Say happy birthday to Beth from us." He handed her the bag with cards and presents.

"I will. Thanks, Dad." She kissed his cheek as instructed and shut the door behind her.

It was set to be a great night, they were going bowling to celebrate Beth's 15th birthday. Tonight was nerve-wracking: Beth, her parents and Rob; her brother, the one Kim really liked. Tonight, she'd meet Beth's new boyfriend too.

Pangs of jealousy stabbed her, but she was happy for her friend. She only hoped this wasn't the end of their evenings together. Many of their classmates abandoned friends once they had boyfriends: she'd miss Beth too much if their friendship was to end now.

Was her top alright? These jeans, they weren't too casual, were they? Her Mum made her smile, saying they showed off her slender figure, and that she looked stunning. She'd confessed her growing liking for Rob, and had been surprised by her mother's advice. Advice that made her head swim.

She could just see how things went tonight. This was Beth's special day, after all.

Chapter 18

Weeks later, Zoe was in deep sedation and Jack looked like he needed sleep when Austin and Yvette arrived at the hospital with Kim and Tom in tow.

Complications had meant a C-section was the best way to deliver the twins. Jack had almost fainted as they cut Zoe open; then he'd been escorted out, despite his protests to remain by his wife's side. Poor Zoe was sobbing in pain when she came round from the operation. Jack could do nothing as she was eased back to sleep, clutching his hand tightly.

Their premature birth meant the tiny twins were breathing with the help of ventilators, but they were here safely. Even Austin agreed as they looked in on the two how gorgeous they were. He couldn't believe how tiny their little fingers and toes were! It almost brought him to tears: swiftly concluding he was getting soft in his old age.

"C'mon you two, let's get home, your father needs some sleep." He smiled at Jack, who looked washed out having been awake all night with Zoe.

"We'll look after you, Dad." Kim said, slipping her hand into his. She'd been upset to see them both in a state and had decided to take charge.

Austin and Yvette smiled as Tom agreed with his sister's statement. Jack fell asleep in the car home, and on the sofa as his teenagers took over. They had the sense to leave him where he was.

Constant ringing of his phone much later that night made them all jump. Jack looked at the clock through half an open eye, groaning at the late time. Who on earth was calling at this time?

Wincing as he tried to get up to answer it - someone had plugged it into charge across the other side of the room, he saw - he was nearly moulded to the sofa. His every muscle hurt from the uncomfortableness as he lumbered across to it.

Suddenly he snapped awake, soon ending the connection.

"What is it?" Tom and Kim were up and downstairs beside him the next moment, both in their slippers and dressing gowns.

Jack grimaced, his phone volume had been turned up loud enough to wake him, but he hadn't wanted to disturb them as well. Mind you, it was a blessing really.

"They want me at the hospital." He was thankful they could look after themselves, not wanting to disturb their friends at such an unGodly hour. "I'll be back when I can. If I'm not back by the time you leave for school, remember to lock the door behind you."

"Yeah, yeah, we will. Just go." Tom ushered him out.

"Okay."

"Be careful." Kim added.

"Okay. See you later, go back to bed. Love you both." And with that he was gone.

It took a few attempts to get the key in the ignition and get the car started; Jack realised he wasn't properly awake yet. Nonetheless, he was by the time he'd rushed up the stairs and through the ward.

Zoe, sobbing and hyperventilating, was fighting the effect of the drugs she was being fed. The sound of her calling his name tore at his heart. Lack of strength weakened her screams and cries: her throat felt raw but she couldn't stop. Immediately, he went to her, holding her tightly.

Jack was talking to her but she couldn't make out his words; ever so slowly, she realised he was there. He winced as Zoe set a vice-like grip around him when she was aware of his presence.

"Zoe, sshhh, it's okay. I'm here now, shhh. It's okay, you're alright. You're alright." His body ached bent over her awkwardly, but he put his pain to one side, knowing he had to calm her down to let the medication work.

It felt like hours before he felt her relax.

"Good girl, that's it Zoe, nice' n easy. You need to rest. You're alright, I'm right here."

He had nearly fallen asleep, holding Zoe in his arms, when she spoke some time later. Jack looked up; seeing a wild look in Zoe's eyes that he didn't like.

"I want to see them."

"No Zoe, you need to rest."

"I do not need to rest. I want to see my babies!" There was a quiet yet angry tone in her voice.

Jack's heart began to pound. He let go of her and backed off before she could grab him again. "Zoe, stop it. Alright? Just stop it."

"If you won't help me, I'll go myself." She swung back the cover and kicked her legs free.

"No, Zoe." He came forward again, holding her shoulders. "You can't. You're not up to that, you're too weak."

"Don't tell me what to do! Get out of my way!" She pushed him with surprising strength.

Jack hit the call button. He grabbed for her as she got to her feet and immediately collapsed in pain. Her weight on top of him forced him to the floor with her, knocking the breath from him, but he kept hold of her until help arrived.

"Mrs Wyndham, what are you doing?" Two nurses had appeared.

"What were you thinking?" The other one said, pulling the cover back over her once they had her back in bed.

Zoe cried herself to sleep.

"Are you alright?" One of them asked.

"Yeah," Jack nodded, holding onto his side, sitting down again.

He could hardly believe what he'd seen. It was almost five in the morning; he'd been here all night again, having been summoned at almost midnight. And Zoe slept as if nothing had happened!

Chapter 19

Kim saw Tom coming from over Beth's shoulder, and was glad of the escape. She pulled a face. Mitch was nothing like she'd thought, and Beth couldn't see his true character, blinded by love.

Tom beckoned to her, and she left, Beth hardly taking any notice, saying 'yeah' without listening. Kim rolled her eyes. As she neared him, Tom turned round and began to walk. She ran to keep up with him; obviously something was wrong.

"Don't worry," she said, "you know Dad said they were all fine."

"I know. It's not that." He sat up on the wall on the quieter side of the building. "Bryony's dumped me."

"What?" She couldn't believe her own ears. "Why?"

"I've seen her hanging around with Al. They're going out, I'm too boring."

"No!"

"I've been laughed at all morning." His expression twisted.

"Oh Tom!" She could see he was on the edge of tears and that shocked her. Tom hadn't even cried when he'd twisted his ankle at football some months ago - and that had hurt for weeks afterwards. "You poor soul." She moved closer, hugging him, surprised to find a muscular frame beneath his baggy clothes.

"I even worked out for her. An' I joined that special maths class. I can't believe it."

"You're too good for her."

Tom half laughed.

"I know it doesn't mean much at the moment, but you'll get

over it. You deserve someone better than her, Tom."

"Yeah," he snivelled.

"Chin up, they'll soon find someone else to take the piss out of." She was glad to see her brother smile.

"Thank you. I needed some comfort - it's PE next."

Kim smiled kindly at him when he looked at her. "Don't think about it. Just go'n beat the crap out of them."

The bell rang to signal the start of the next lesson: lunch always went quickly. Agreeing to meet at their normal time and place, they then went their separate ways. Dear Tom, she loved him.

If only she could find herself a mate like him.... Well, she did have a mate like him, she smiled at Rob as she took her seat in the class; it was more than a mate she wanted.

"Right, people. I want you to work in pairs - of my choosing, so don't get comfy."

Kim tried to hide her grin as she was placed as Rob's partner. It was Biology, normally a boring subject, but Kim simply flew through the coursework. So much so, she had been placed in the class above her age grade – Rob's class.

She was headed for a top award, provided she kept up the good work. These words rang in her head throughout every lesson, and she was determined to meet that expectation. Her stubbornness was one of the traits she'd inherited from her father.

She could hardly believe her eyes when Rob passed her a note, under the textbook they were sharing. When she read the first line, she almost stopped.

Can I see you, at break, alone?

Her heart pounded - why the secrecy? Did he know that she liked him? Did he have feelings for her? She forced herself to read on.

I want your advice about Beth and Mitch. Please.

She glanced at him, and was surprised to find he was looking into her eyes. She nodded and so did he. She couldn't decide if she was relieved or disappointed.

By mid morning, Zoe was much improved. Upset at the knowledge that Jack was hurt, and it was her fault, she was more than confused that she had no recollection of the night's happenings.

"I've really hurt him," she said quietly, watching as Austin accompanied Jack for an examination.

Yvette squeezed her hand. "It wasn't your fault, Zoe. You didn't do it on purpose." She continued. "He'll be alright. They'll patch him up."

Zoe dissolved into tears, unable to believe what had happened. Yvette did her best to comfort her friend, hoping that her words would ring true and Jack would be alright.

A while later, Austin put his head round the door, attracting Yvette's attention. He mouthed, 'was she alright to stay while he took Jack home for some rest?' Yvette nodded. Only then did he come into the room properly, kissing Yvette then Zoe.

"I'm gonna take Jack home, but I'll be back as soon as he's settled." He told them.

"Aus," Zoe grabbed his hand.

"Don't worry, he's alright. He just wants to sleep before coming back tonight. I'll be back before you know it." He squeezed Zoe's hand before she let go of him.

Yvette nodded again. "You're alright, Zoe. Everybody's okay." She stroked her friend's hair, remembering how soothing it felt for her. "Just relax."

"Eve,"

"Uh-huh,"

"Gone tired again." She murmured, closing her eyes.

A quick glance reassured Yvette that her friend's stats were fine. "Yeah, that's alright Zoe. Have a sleep. We'll be here when you wake up again."

"Promise?"

"Promise." She smiled at her friend, not wishing to trade places for the world. "You poor thing, get some rest."

"Eve?" Austin was back in a flash. He spoke quietly, seeing Zoe was asleep.

Her face lit up when she saw him: it always did. Cuddling and kissing her then, he checked nothing had occurred since he'd left.

"You okay?"

"Yeah. Is Jack alright?"

"Mmm... a few cracked ribs."

"Ouch." Yvette winced.

"Yeah, but he's okay, painkillers soon put him out. Left him at ours, and said I'd come back to pick him up for the evening visiting time."

Yvette nodded. "That was wise."

They share a smile.

"Is she alright?" Austin turned his concern to a now slumbering Zoe.

"They gave her something to help her sleep. Poor thing. She's distraught at the idea she's hurt him."

It was Austin's turn to nod. "The doctor reckons it'll be a few days before they can go home."

"Good. Give them all a chance to recover. The twins are doing great, so they'll be able to go home together."

Nodding, Austin hugged Yvette then, glad that they could help their friends in such a small way. He was sure they'd be a help to the family a fair bit over the next few weeks.

Yvette squeezed Austin, so glad to have married a man

who was always able to take control of the situation. She smiled as he dropped a kiss on her head, as he was prone to doing.

Arriving home to an empty house, the answering machine flashing, Tom pressed the playback button and he and Kim listened carefully. Both of them heaved a sigh of relief together. Another microwave meal in front of the TV; it was becoming a regular treat.   They worked together and were soon sitting down to eat. Completing that night's homework relatively quickly, they found a TV programme they both liked and sat down to relax.

When Jack came home, they were watching the news before going to bed. It was nearly eleven by the time he had relayed everything to them and they all fell into bed simultaneously.

What seemed like not long later, there was knocking on the door. Bleary eyed, Jack looked at the clock and groaned.

"Dad?"

"Yeah?"

Kim stuck her head round the door, and he smiled, beckoning her in. His smile widened when he saw she'd brought him tea and toast. "Thought you'd be awake by now - we're going soon."

Jack yawned, carefully, trying not to stretch too much as it pulled his sore ribs. "Thanks, Kim. You okay?"

"I'm fine. I don't think Tom is though." Jack looked at her questionably. "He didn't want to tell you himself. He and Bryony broke up yesterday, and he's a bit upset. Not that he'll show it."

Jack groaned again, this time for a different reason.

"She says he's boring and now she's going out with another guy from their year."

Jack grimaced, recalling a father-son conversation they'd had only recently. She seemed like a nice girl too. "Plenty more fish in the sea."

"That's what I said. Poor Tom. Anyway, best go or we'll be late. Are we going to the hospital tonight?"

"Yeah. I'll pick you both up, normal place and time, okay?" He paused as she nodded. "Thanks, Kim. Keep an eye on him. Have a nice day."

He smiled as she kissed his cheek and left him to it, hearing the reassuring click of the door closing behind them.

They were growing up so fast. Jack smiled to himself, and now there were another two to nurture: not that the nurturing ended for Tom and Kim; nurturing never ended.

Chapter 20

It'd been a long time since she was a footballer's wife, sitting watching the battle unravel in front of her. It's funny how life goes, Yvette reflected. Obviously Austin was destined to be a footballer, in one way or another.

The previous month Austin had been successful at the school's charity match - he played at Tom's suggestion as Jack had his hands rather full. What they hadn't known was that one of the spectators had a senior team, the Premiers, in one of the minor indoor five-a-side leagues. Bob was on the lookout for new players at all times, and highly impressed by what he saw.

As there was due a story in the local paper, Austin brushed up on a few tricks and techniques with Tom beforehand. It'd been hard work and Yvette laughed often as her "star" was reduced to laughter when things didn't go his way. Tom seemed quite disappointed the first few times, but knowing a thing or two, geed his Uncle up. Austin rewarded Tom's patience with his rusty footwork by showing good form at the match.

Even Bob, owner and manager of the Premiers, had been surprised as the nutmegs found success time and time again. He smiled to himself: a striker had been found. He agreed with Austin that he was right to put Yvette first and it was made clear that the team was in no way regimented.

So here they were.

Bob's wife, Helen, Yvette couldn't help feeling had been pressed to accompany her. Helen, like Bob, oozed charm but not in an over the top way. She was open and friendly, and Yvette found herself taking an instant liking to her.

The best thing, Helen confided, was that being indoors eradicated the need for hot flasks of tea on the touchline in the pouring rain. Yvette laughed, able to remember those days.

Indoor five-a-side took a bit of adjustment from normal football, even for Austin who proclaimed that he'd be rusty for a while. The first few sessions, he constantly checked on Yvette, from afar and at half time, gradually trusting her reassurance. Once settled, he made waves.

The self-assured guys in defence soon had the wind knocked out of their sails, Austin's favourite trick catching them out for the first few training sessions. Although they didn't seem to know about a nutmeg, there was hope for them.

Last season they had performed average and Bob dreamed of Premier League promotion, hence his excitement at Austin's discovery. How fitting promotion would be for the team, this season re-named 'the Premiers'.

Their next opponents were last season's second-top performers, the Stingers, (the top team having achieved promotion), and were as rough as they came. They were big guys: Austin and some of the Premiers team were six footers, but these guys were big both ways.

Yvette could not hide her anxiety: Austin caught the vibes and plotted with Bob that if it got too rough, he would be substituted. The last thing anyone wanted was to trigger Yvette's downfall: no Yvette meant no Austin, and Bob was already relying on his new striker.

The Stingers had heard about Bob's star "signing" and it wasn't long before a goal against them rattled their cages; Austin set up perfectly for his strike partner Andy to score. Yvette screwed her eyes closed as she watched Austin be the victim of a terrible foul. At the blowing of the whistle, she opened her eyes to see him picking himself out of the net. Bob was doing his nut on the sidelines, and a penalty was rightfully awarded. "Did you see that?!" Bob turned to Helen and Yvette.

"I couldn't watch." Yvette didn't take her eyes off Austin as he came across the hall to them: Helen was famed for tea and antiseptic spray.

"Are you alright?" Helen asked him, knowing this was what Yvette wanted to know as well.

"Yeah, I'm fine... Ow!" Antiseptic stung the graze across his knee but soon he was off again, giving Yvette a reassuring nod: that was his penalty and he was determined to take it.

Yvette smiled to herself, she'd forgotten how determined he was. That very moment, she prayed he wouldn't get seriously hurt.

Austin perhaps over-hit the shot, his blast hit the wall behind the goal before flying back out, causing everybody to laugh.

2-0, what a great start to the match! Bob's grin was there for all to see.

The Stingers were blocking with their bodies, and there was not a lot any of the Premiers could do to get past. The team members were everywhere, from upfront to defending the goal line: several goal attempts were blocked, and not just by Phil in the Premiers' goal.

After several agonising minutes of added time, the final whistle blew. The Premiers team jumped on Austin with delight, while Bob grinned from ear to ear. The Stingers were not amused, on their way out muttering they'd win the title regardless.

"We'll see about that." Bob jeered back, shutting the door behind them, signalling to Helen that it was time to go.

Yvette pulled a face as she received a sweaty hug, smiling

as all the team, those that played and those sat were subs, all patted Austin on the back and offered congratulations.

"Well done you." She said, kissing him.

Austin shrugged. "It was nothin'."

"Don't undermine this. Helen was telling me the odds of the top two at the end of the season being tonight's line up. We're pretty much favourite now."

Austin grinned, secretly pleased that Yvette had taken so much of an interest. For a while at least, it took her away from her own troubles.

She sent him off to shower, waiting by the centre entrance for him. Quizzing Helen and Bob on what would happen if they achieved promotion, Helen laughed, replying they'd think about it when it happened.

That was fair enough, Yvette replied, but would terms change? Bob reassured her that she'd be involved in the discussions, as and when they happened. Yvette accepted this. She could see the team going far, if things went to plan.

"Well done, Austin." Helen congratulated him when he reappeared.

"Not bad for a debut." He smiled at Helen and Bob, kissing Yvette. "C'mon then, back to reality."

They laughed and headed out together alone: the rest of the team had already left for their normal lives.

Chapter 21

Morale hit a low. This game was over before it had started, on paper. The City Bears were newly formed and unprepared for such battles, or so they all thought. So, it must have been beginner's luck, for the Premiers were 3-1 down by half-time.

A change in the playing schedule meant the next match was in a few days and Bob, quite rightly, wanted to save Andy and Austin for the more important of the two. Didn't that serve him right for underestimating the other team!

Austin's grazed knee had stiffened up and he'd chosen the subs bench before Bob had made the decision.

"C'mon guys, the way we're playing it's like you've gone home already. Pull yourselves together." Bob chastised them.

Austin could feel their bad vibes, deciding to try to inject some positivity. "Phil, don't get disheartened, you're doing an excellent job. Remember, you can't keep everything out. Steve and Paul, work together, we're a team not individuals. We need to tighten it up."

He outlined a plan, and with that, they went out.

Bob moaned as the team filed back out onto the floor. "What an embarrassment!"

"Give them time. We can still do it. You've gotta keep encouraging them, it's no good putting them down. Making them feel worse won't work, we're too old for reverse psychology."

Bob hid his amusement and surprise. Austin then told him about his playing days with Jack, and everything fell into place - including the idea of Jack as his replacement, should the need ever arise.

Thanks largely to Austin's pep talk, they finished with a draw. With only ten teams in each division playing every fortnight, the season was strung out. Still, a draw was a good result in any league – far better than a loss!

"You know I cannot promise anything." Austin folded his arms across his chest.

"I know, but I need to plan a team - if we're promoted, we'll need to do more training and more fitness."

"It depends how much more is, and how flexible our arrangement is. Yvette comes first, I told you that in the beginning." Austin was angry to think that Bob was trying to force the issue they had already discussed. He changed the subject. "Anyway, we don't know we'll be promoted."

"Of course we will." Bob looked up at him, shocked.

"There's a big fall to be had from big expectations. You can't get hurt if the jump's not high in the first place."

Bob nodded gravely, knowing he was right. "I want to take you on as Assistant, but I know you cannot promise anything. The regulations board wants me to name the team, and an Assistant Manager, if we're promoted. They're sceptical."

Austin shrugged. "Let them come down and see what we've got going on then."

The grin threatened to split Bob's face.

It was strange to be at the next match without Yvette. Austin had taken a lot of persuading to leave her behind.

Although she didn't feel right, she didn't feel that unwell either, so they agreed that he would go to the match, with Jack watching over her. Zoe was of course at home with the twins, and Kim and Tom.

He tried to ignore the feeling that something was wrong in the pit of his stomach: he knew Yvette was right to send him out for a distraction. If she was coming down with something, it might be a while before he was able to play for the team again...

No more than five minutes in, Bob substituted him.

"What's going on?" Austin jogged over, tagging his replacement.

The expression on Bob's face said it all. "I'm sorry Austin, you're needed at the hospital."

Oh God, no...

Mentally he kicked himself, Yvette had said she was fine; she'd insisted on him going. He should have trusted his gut instinct to not leave...

"Austin, go." Bob squeezed his shoulder, snapping him from his thoughts. "Let us know how she is."

Austin caught himself in time, nearly erupting. Biting back the sobs in the back of his throat, he nodded. Running out of the hall and out of the centre, he was soon out of the car park, aware he was driving too fast and slowing a fraction.

"Where is she?" He ran in, through the waiting room, up to the desk.

The receptionist was on the phone, agreed a few times and tapped in another few appointments: Austin waited impatiently.

"Name?" She said when she'd finished.

"Yvette Leigh," Austin spoke almost breathlessly.

The receptionist nodded, tapping in Yvette's details and relaying that she was in IC.

Intensive Care.

Colour drained from Austin's face so quickly, she thought he was going to pass out. Quickly, he turned on his heel, knowing the way without needing directions.

"You can't go in, they're examining her." Jack caught his arm before he could barge into the special ward.

"What happened?"

"I don't know." Jack admitted, letting his breath out slowly. "She was okay one minute and fighting for breath the next. I called for help and we were here, they dragged me out not long ago."

Austin sank to the floor. "I knew I shouldn't have left her."

Jack crouched down beside him. "There was nothing you could've done, Aus, even if you had been there."

Seeing him in tears, he was stunned into silence, wondering how he was going to cope with what was happening, never mind what might happen next...

"Austin!" He leapt to his feet after him, chasing him through the heavy double doors.

The sight in front of them stopped him in his tracks. One of the nurses had wrestled a now hysterical Austin into a chair on the other side of the room. The piercing sound of the heart monitor echoing in his ears: Jack was sure it was something he would never forget.

Austin's cries were barely audible over it, the dreadful sounds filled Jack's ears no matter how much he tried to block them out. Without realising quite what he had seen, the medical professionals were trying to restart Yvette's heart with the defibrillator.

Allowing him to lean on his shoulder, Jack put his arms around Austin's shaking body, silently willing. "Thank God." The words slipped out of his mouth without him realising when he heard the all clear.

A nurse stood over them, speaking to them. "Mr Leigh?"

Jack looked up, realising he too was in tears. "No, that's him."

She nodded, giving him a small, kind smile. "We've stablised her and made sure she'll rest. The doctor will be round to check on her again later. The monitors are on view next door, I'll keep an eye on her from there."

Jack was confused. "So soon?"

"She's been stable for an hour now."

"Oh." Jack realised they'd totally lost track of time. Poor Austin was a wreck.

"There's a strong chance she can hear us."

Jack nodded. "Okay, thank you." He squeezed Austin. "Aus?"

"It's my fault!" Austin sobbed.

"Oh Austin!" He squeezed him tighter. "No, it's not. Poor Yvette's not well. But she's much better now - she must be, they're monitoring her from afar now. That's a good sign."

Austin nodded, pulling away from him to slowly make his way to the bedside. He was shaking so much, he couldn't take Yvette's hand, instead dissolving into tears again.

Jack took hold of him by the shoulders to steer him into a chair by the bed, squatting down beside him. He swallowed hard as Austin's words reverberated around his head.

"She died. Jack, she died."

"I know, Aus." He had a fleeting thought of Zoe, poor Zoe; he'd left her a message to say that he was going to the hospital with Yvette. "Eve's a fighter. We all know she is."

Allowing Jack to hug him again, Austin tried to fight the reeling of his emotions. Getting to his feet suddenly, he fled the room.

Jack soon caught up with him in the corridor, where he had stopped, having been violently sick. "I think he needs something." He said to the nurse who'd arrived at the scene.

"Aus, it's alright. It's the shock." He rubbed Austin's back, his heart pounding as he squatted down again beside Austin as he sat on the floor. The thought struck Jack then. "He's diabetic, I don't know when he had his last shot, but he probably needs one."

Thankful that they had a hospital full of capable staff, Jack wasn't sure he could deal with this situation as it started to spiral out of his control. He prayed Zoe wouldn't arrive then... bless her, poor Zoe was in no position to help.

"Aus? Are you still with us?" He squeezed his nearest shoulder, relieved when Austin nodded. He'd long since closed his eyes. "You're not staying here, I'm taking you home with me. Yvette won't know any difference. She's safe here. We'll come back in the morning, okay?"

Austin nodded, too wiped out to form any sort of argument. The scene replayed over and over in his mind; his poor Yvette taking her last breath... He needed Jack to do the thinking for him, he knew then.

"Take him home and give him these."

Jack nodded at the doctor's instructions. "What about his blood sugar? What should I do?"

He nodded, memorising further instructions.

How would he get Zoe round this? There was no other option, he wouldn't forgive himself if something happened to Austin as well as Yvette.

Despite telling Austin there was nothing he could have done, he didn't believe his own words, sure that somewhere, somehow, he'd missed something that caused their friends' latest heartache. Guilt consumed him.

Chapter 22

"What will you have for breakfast?" Jack tried.

Austin shook his head.

"But Aus, you must eat. And you've got to eat before you take your medication." Zoe added.

Austin had been asleep virtually since Jack arrived home with him, supporting him. It was obvious that he needed the rest. The medication Jack had pocketed as he'd got Austin to his feet twelve hours previously had, thankfully, worked.

"Would you two stop ganging up on me." Austin's frown deepened.

"We're only concerned." Zoe said quietly.

Austin rubbed his head. "I know, I know, I'm sorry."

She came closer, and opened her arms to him, beckoning him for a hug.

He put his arms around her. "I'm sorry, Zoe. I'm not used to having a fuss made over me." Smiling at Jack over her shoulder, he realised he was relieved Jack had forced him to be looked after. "What did you all have? It smells wonderful."

"Fresh orange and croissants, with hot butter melted all over them." Jack returned his smile.

"Sounds great to me. I'll do it though, you two have other things to do."

Zoe squeezed him and got up. "No, it's okay, you stay there."

"But..."

"But nothing, Aus." She cut him off. "Tom and Kim left for school ages ago, and the twins are asleep, having kept us awake most the night." Jack and Zoe smiled at each other. "I'm surprised you didn't hear them."

"Didn't hear anything." Austin shrugged.

"You must've needed the rest." Zoe tousled his hair and headed to the kitchen.

Austin leant over, picking up the little bottle from the table. He caught Jack's eye. "Is this what you gave me last night?" Jack nodded, watching as he read the label.

Austin closed his eyes in disbelief, putting it back down. "I've tried to keep control."

"You can't all the time. I don't know how you deal with everything."

"What d'you mean?"

"How you deal with Yvette's conditions, and yours. How you always manage to stay on top of things."

Austin nodded, but didn't speak.

"I'm surprised you haven't been carted off to the nut house by now." Jack tried to joke, glad to see Austin smile.

But the smile didn't last long. "I can't do it anymore." Austin's voice came out as a whisper.

Zoe had slipped back into the room unnoticed. She stopped dead when she heard not specifically what Austin said, but how he said it.

Something snapped within him.

Jack rattled the pill pot. "These'll sort it out."

Austin shook his head.

"Aus, trust me. We've both been there."

Zoe came into the room properly, taking hold of Austin's hand. "We'll help you, Aus."

"There's no miracle of modern science." Austin shook his head slowly. "There's nothing that can help Yvette."

"Yes, there is." Jack tried to argue.

"Not fully." The cold truth in his words brought a chill into the room.

Zoe couldn't get her head round this. She looked at Jack,

puzzled and, though she wouldn't readily admit it, frightened.

Rob shook his head. "I don't like him. What about you?"

"I don't know him." Kim said truthfully. She could see this was not what Rob had wanted her to say. "But there's something I don't like about him. He's not..." she stopped.

"He's not what?"

She shook her head.

"C'mon, tell me,"

"He's not... I dunno, it sounds silly, but he's not the sort of boyfriend I imagined her to have. And she's changed." Kim stopped, looking at his expression. "I've been replaced, it's hard to describe."

"I know, I've been replaced too, we never used to have any secrets."

Alarm bells rang in Kim's head. "No secrets?"

He shook his head. "Surely you and Tom are the same? You're very close."

"I wouldn't say we have no secrets, but we are close."

Rob noticed the way that the smile found her lips when she spoke of her brother. It was obvious that their bond ran deep. He suspected this deepened when their parents had that rift... yes he knew about that too, what Kim had briefly told him herself, Beth had filled the blanks in.

He was glad in a way, because it had brought them to this part of the world and their friendship was one that strengthened slowly. You just know when you find a special friend. And he had that feeling. He swallowed hard, the second reason for wanting peace with her coming to the forefront of his mind.

"Can I ask you something?"

Kim's heart began to pound. "Yes, of course you can."

"It's our cousin Di's wedding next weekend. Beth's taking

Mitch, would you come along with me. I mean, we could keep an eye on them? And who knows, it might be fun."

Kim smiled to herself. His hesitation was a sign that her mother had told her to watch out for. Did it mean he was embarrassed to go to the wedding and didn't want to be alone, or did it mean that he wanted her to go?

"I'll have to ask, but I don't see why not. Where is it?"

"I've written it down." As he handed her the piece of paper, their hands touched briefly.

Kim's heart fluttered. At that moment, the bell rang and they jumped to their feet. "I'll phone, tonight, when I've asked."

"Okay, see you later?"

"Yeah, see you later."

"Ooh! Going for the smart guy, eh?" Louise came up behind her, having seen the exchange.

"Y'what?"

"You're hot for him."

"We're friends." Kim said, immediately wishing her face would stop burning.

"Ooh... Kim and Rob! I'm gonna ask where he's taking you for your first date!" She teased; the look on Kim's face said everything.

"Leave him alone, just because he's nice."

"And quiet. It's the quiet ones you gotta watch, y'know."

Kim walked faster, getting to their class before Louise's teasing got to her. She was so looking forward to the weekend. Teasing the paper open, she read what he'd written. She smiled when she read his words, how he "hoped she could come".

He wanted her there! Beth was just an excuse. She couldn't help but feel victorious.

Chapter 23

There were near miracles, however.

A mere ten weeks later, Yvette managed to persuade Austin to participate in the team's next match. Their challenge for the top slot had taken a drastic nose dive, for many reasons. The difference Austin's presence made could be felt by everyone, he held so much respect amongst the team.

They all knew that he couldn't be counted upon for every game and changes had to be made. That was the difference between this league and the professional ones.

Austin agreed to participate only for half the match, anxious as to how Yvette would cope not only being out of bed, but in a totally different environment. They'd all been warned not to make any fuss; Helen especially promised to keep a tactful eye on her whilst he played.

Austin had re-discovered his grip on the edge over the weeks, largely due to his responsibilities: he wouldn't put anyone before Yvette, never mind himself!

Yvette knew, he hadn't wanted her involved, but she knew everything. They always had a tender and loving partnership, even before the incidents one after another, that would have torn apart most other couples.

But Austin's passion wasn't in it. His stride faltered. He played a different game, setting them up but not going for glory himself. Defending, he made uncharacteristic errors and gave away several fouls.

Phil found himself nose-to-nose with his opponent. Austin got in between the two, sensing a fight around the hypothetical corner, and the other man tried to swing at him.

Phil's rage boiled over and soon had the bigger man pinned against the wall. "People like you need to be taught a lesson. Austin's here to have a game with us, to keep some spirit in our hearts. His poor wife over there is a very sick young lady and you should hold the same respect we do. If you want to fight, you and I will fight, but don't touch him." Seeing the hang-dog expression on his face, Phil then put the man down again.

Austin was impressed, despite himself. This had been the first time ever someone had come to his rescue, someone outside of their friends. At half time, he headed straight over to Helen and Yvette, seeing Yvette was ghostly white. As he went to pull away from their hug, Yvette didn't let go of him. His heart began to pound.

"Eve? You're not alright, are you?"

Slowly, Yvette shook her head.

"I think it's a bit too much too soon." He saw Helen nodding in agreement. "It's different being at home, to being out. We'll go home." He frowned, the flinching across Yvette's expression worrying.

"My chest hurts." She whispered.

"Uh-huh, I know sweetheart, and you're tired. It's taken a lot out of you. You've done well to recover so much in so little time."

Weakly, she nodded.

"Perhaps I should drive you," Helen offered: Austin looked up. "Then you could keep an eye on her."

"But how would I get the car home?"

"I mean, I'll drive your car. Bob can pick me up, the game will soon be over - the second half starts soon."

"Are you sure?"

"Yes, I'll tell Bob. You get sorted, I'll see you back at your car." Austin nodded, his expression betraying his relief. "You are okay to go home now, aren't you Yvette?" She checked, turning to Yvette, who also nodded.

With that, she set off.

They hadn't been home long before Helen spoke his thoughts. "I don't mean to intrude," she began, "you know what's best, but shouldn't we call a doctor?"

Poor Yvette's chest felt so tight, her breaths were rattling. She hadn't been this bad for weeks. Her inhalers had made a slight difference, so they knew it wasn't an asthma issue.

Austin shrugged. "I don't think there's much any doctor can do."

Helen nodded at the truth in his words, but she couldn't help worrying. She was glad when Bob arrived.

"What exactly is wrong?" He asked gently.

"They thought it's this virus, I can't remember what they called it but it's pretty lethal. It has a similar effect to the flu, and obviously Eve's in the high risk group. But there's no vaccinations yet, they barely know how to contain it and what damage it does."

Bob and Helen nodded gravely, both unsure of what to say next.

"Are you okay, or do you want us to stay?" Helen offered a few minutes of silence later.

Austin smiled. "Thanks, but we'll be okay."

"Sure?" Helen asked.

"Sure, thanks."

"Keep us updated, alright?" Bob asked, aware that Austin hadn't updated him the last time he'd requested such.

Austin nodded, and the couple slipped out silently. Yvette had drifted off into a light sleep he noticed with relief, her breathing easing.

An hour into the after ceremony party, dancing in full swing; Rob beckoned Kim to follow him outside. Beth and Mitch were on the dance floor with Di and her new husband, Tyrone. It was safe to leave for a minute, no-one would notice their absence.

They went out, ducking under the other marquee, where it was quiet. The light rain lay in beads on Kim's hair and on the shoulders of her dress.

Rob grinned at her. "You look stunning, y'know."

"You don't look so bad yourself." She teased, trying to calm her beating heart.

"I wanted to talk to you."

Here comes, Kim thought to herself.

"I...I think you're very special, Kim." He took a deep breath. "I'd like it if you'd be mine."

Kim was stunned at the short delivery, unable to hide her grin. He took her hands as he shuffled closer to her, looking directly into her eyes. Kim felt herself melt. As they were about to kiss, they leapt apart at the sound of footsteps and laughter.

"It's Di," he whispered, "they've probably come looking for us."

"Sshh." Kim tried.

They could hear every word, and were so amazed they couldn't believe their ears. Rob still had hold of her hand, and didn't let go. The newlyweds had escaped for some peace and quiet of their own.

Kim couldn't decide if she was horrified or humiliated. From where they were, nothing could be seen, but plenty could be heard. The zip had been drawn so that the flaps were closed and the pair were at it on one of the tables. She dared to look across at Rob. He too wore the same facial expression; mixed horror and fascination.

He felt jealous of the man, and the sounds they were making made his imagination run riot. In his dreams, public sex turned him on. Kim had similar thoughts. She felt the urge to kiss him, at long last, to find out what it felt like to kiss. A proper kiss. She smiled and turned to him, pressing her lips against his, just briefly. She liked it.

She did it again, this time for a bit longer. Rob put his arms around her and she likewise, hugging him, squeezing him tight. He felt so scrawny and bony. Next time as they kissed, his tongue found hers. At first she was so surprised, she pulled back. It was a strange sensation.

"I'm sorry." He whispered.

"It's okay. Do it again." She whispered back, the feeling was growing on her and she realised that she too could move her tongue. So, this was what a real kiss was! She shivered as he ran his hands down her back. It was a pleasurable shiver. She copied his action.

They pulled away as Di screamed, and again, a raw passionate scream; Tyrone was moaning too. Rob looked around them, and spied a loose tent peg. He indicated it to her and they left. Why hadn't he noticed that before?

"Are you alright?" he said.

"Yeah - you?"

"Yeah, I'll be back in a minute. Will you be here?"

"Of course." Kim smiled, sitting down carefully and drawing her chair under the table, now back in the main tent.

She noticed the drink was flowing freely and everyone was having a good time; but not half as much as Di and Tyrone were, she smiled to herself. Lucky buggers. Still, she resolved, one day that would be her: happy and married, and having great sex. She hoped it would be with Rob.

She smiled as he returned with a drink for them both; a

straight Coke for her, she hadn't touched alcohol since that night with Beth. How sick she'd been, not that she'd told her friend this. Funnily enough, no-one knew except Rob. And then the realisation dawned on her. What if it went wrong: their friendship would be ruined.

Rob squeezed her hand under the table and her heart fluttered. No, this wasn't going to go wrong. But love did make you blind, she knew. Looking around them, her eye fell on Beth.

She was alone. And tearful. She beckoned to Kim to come over to her. Rob stood up to go with her, but Kim told him to stay, it was probably for the best, and she'd signal to him if they wanted him.

"Please Kim, please tell me I've done the right thing." Tears slid down her face.

"What are you talking about?" Kim's eyes narrowed with suspicion.

Beth sniffed. "He...he wanted to make out and I said no, and ...and he got annoyed, and so I said it was over and he stormed out."

"Of course you did the right thing." Kim hugged her then. "I didn't think he was good for you."

"Neither did I." Rob added from behind them.

Beth turned a shade of pink, to think that her own brother had heard her say that!

"I'm proud of you." Kim continued.

Beth sniffed. "But I'm nearly sixteen, there's loadsa people doing it."

"If loadsa people jumped off a bridge, you wouldn't join them, would you?"

Beth shook her head.

"Well, there you go then." Kim was glad to see her friend smile. She looked at Rob and they reached the same conclusion: they couldn't tell Beth about them, not today, it would rub salt in her wounds.

"You deserve better than him." Rob said gently. "Here," he handed her a drink, "this'll make you feel better, it's your favourite."

Chapter 24

"Hey, how're you doing?"

Austin returned her quiet greeting. "Hey Zoe,"

She was wearing a frown. "I would've come sooner, only Thirza didn't let me in."

He smiled briefly. "I didn't want you either catching or transporting the germs to your lot. Especially with the twins."

"I know, I realised that."

He looked drained, but still had Yvette cradled in his arms as usual. Yvette didn't wake, not even when Zoe sat on the bench beside them.

"It's a bad one for both of you to have caught the same virus."

Austin nodded, stifling his yawn. On top of the mystery flu-type virus, Yvette had developed a nasty viral infection. With his immune system susceptible anyway thanks to the diabetes and the everyday stress, it was only a matter of time before Austin too fell victim to it, and had to call in their hired help.

It was nice out here, Zoe could see why they were not indoors, fed up of being cooped up for the week that they had both been ill. Just warm enough to see the sun shining off the sea and hear the waves making their magical sounds.

"Oh Eve, I didn't mean to wake you babe." Zoe gently hugged her friends as Yvette stirred.

"Zoe," Yvette's breathing immediately turned wheezy.

"It's okay, babe." She rubbed Yvette's chest, listening horrified as her wheezing increased.

"Promise me," she began, "you will... look after him ...if I die,"

"Yvette!" Zoe was so shocked she almost let go of her. She saw Austin shared her shock: for a moment, he didn't react, although he had her inhaler on him, in case something like this happened... She re-secured her grip around her. "I will, but you're not going anywhere."

Austin nodded his agreement, soothing Yvette into taking her medication, hoping it would quickly work.

She was almost sandwiched between the pair of them; but she didn't mind. It felt good to be between the two people she loved most.

As he hoped, she did calm, and reasonably quickly. Murmuring how tired she felt, Austin made his decision.

"C'mon Eve, let's go back to bed."

Following them through the house, Zoe hadn't quite realised how lucky her family were to be fully fit and healthy: there and then, she prayed this would remain so throughout their lives. Slipping the duvet over them, as Austin lay beside Yvette on his side, kissing and soothing her, she sat down on the bed beside them.

The slight colour he had regained had since faded again, and within minutes Yvette was sleeping, although even her resting breaths wheezy. Zoe found herself glad she knew the pattern for their help, relieved that Thirza would be back to stay for the night with the pair. She snapped back out of her thoughts when Austin spoke.

His expression was woeful. "She's my everything,"

Zoe's heart melted. "I know, Aus. I wouldn't have let you take her away otherwise." She was pleased to see him smile with her jest. "I'll stay 'til Thirza comes back, it's not long now, is it?"

He glanced at the clock, shaking his head.

"Good. Now, get some rest. Eve's alright."

"No,"

"Yes." She cut off his protest. "You've gone pale again. Are you feeling alright?"

Austin sighed. "Just a bit... washed out."

"Uh-huh, that's to be expected. Have a rest. Eve's out for the count."

He nodded, knowing what she said made perfect sense. Quietly, he was relieved that Zoe had been determined to visit, and promised to stay for a while longer.

Kim and Rob grinned at each other, alone at his house as everybody was out for the evening. There was chill out music on and candles lit the room.

"Tell me what feels good."

"Okay." Her heart was pounding.

They were nearly naked, only in their underwear. It's just a massage, calm down, nothing's going to happen. So, why did she feel so terrified?

"Is that okay, I don't want to hurt you?" Rob could feel the tension coming from her in waves, hoping that he would help her to relax. He rubbed her shoulders and her neck, moving slowly down her back.

"No, that's fine. Mmm, that feels good."

It was such a relief to let Beth in on their relationship, there was nothing to hide now. Neither of their parents had said much, just to be careful - and they knew what that meant. There were so many teenage pregnancies now, they were warned not to become a statistic.

Kim wasn't ready for sex, and she'd told him this. The idea scared her, if she was to be truthful with herself. Rob, to his credit, was prepared to wait until she was ready.

"Can I undo this? It's in the way."

He wants to undo my bra... For a moment or two, Kim couldn't find her tongue.

"Kim, you're not falling asleep are you?"

"No,"

"Can I undo your bra, or do you want to keep it on?"

"You can undo it."

"Are you sure?"

"Yeah." She closed her eyes, praying that he was as good as his word. He'd said that he wouldn't do anything she didn't want him to.

Rob had picked up a few tricks from his relationship research, like the massage and relaxing music. Although she was a year behind everyone else in their class, this didn't make any difference where he was concerned. He'd come to realise that he loved her, and though they were only young, he didn't want anyone else. So if she wanted to take it slow, that would be what they would do. There was no hurry: they had all of their lives. Or so he hoped.

He skipped from her back and neck to her legs, his fingers slowly making their way higher up her thigh.

"Does it feel good? It felt good when you were doing it to me."

Did he just say what I thought he just said? Kim's eyes widened and she was glad for a moment that they weren't face to face.

Rob had the same thought, and quickly added: "The massage, that is. It feels really good."

"It does."

He lay on the bed, beside her and they cuddled. It was a funny sensation, being skin-to-skin. She couldn't help but laugh when she felt.... is that what I think it is?

Rob too laughed, more out of embarrassment. "I can't help it, when he's alert, he's alert. And you make him alert." He caught the frightened look on her face. "But don't worry, he knows he must wait. And he'll wait as long as he has to."

"I want to." Kim said quietly, drawing in a deep breath. "But it scares me. But, I want to, so I'm torn." She frowned.

Reassuringly, he nodded and hugged her. "I know. We'll know when it's right."

Kim nodded, relieved he was understanding and didn't force her into anything. She jumped to her feet, seeing what the time was.

"What's wrong?"

"I didn't know it was so late. I should be home."

She hastily got back into her clothes and for the first time he saw her naked, from the waist up anyway. He was both stunned and ashamed of how he felt at the same time.

Loudly, he cleared his throat. "Okay. No hurry. I'll walk you home."

"Sure?"

"God yes, I'm not letting you walk home alone, it's dark out."

"You're a gentleman." She smiled, leaning over to kiss him.

"I know you're alright when you're with me."

Kim was blown away by these simple words. They proved how deep his feelings ran. She'd been warned that guys didn't show feelings and emotions like the girls did. But he was different, and that was why she felt the way she did about him.

Chapter 25

"Go on, open it."

Zoe smiled, unsure of what the envelope contained. It seemed like a strange birthday present... but then again, that all depended on what the small envelope contained. There were tickets inside: four tickets for a long weekend in Edinburgh, and theatre tickets tucked behind them.

She frowned. "What about Tom and Kim?"

"I did ask, they said they didn't want to come."

"Oh."

Zoe sounded so disappointed, Jack felt he had to continue. "And it's too near the exams to be taking them out of school."

Zoe nodded; that was true. Jack hugged her and she smiled.

"It's an ideal time to go, before the twins go to school. And before you go back."

Yes, she almost dreaded the idea of going back to help out again at the school. It felt like many years since the first time. She smiled, thinking back those years.

Life had passed them by so quickly in the almost five years that they had been in Cornwall. Tom was at college now, in his first year: Kim was doing her exams, hopefully to get herself to college, though she wasn't sure what to do just yet. There was plenty of time for her to decide.

Zoe couldn't help but be surprised when Tom said he was going to study nursing. She almost laughed when she caught the look on Jack's face - nursing was not considered a manly career and Jack frowned upon this idea. However, after a man-to-man chat, he found out all he needed to know, and Tom convinced him.

When they thought about it, Tom was perfect for a nursing role. He was patient and understanding; he dealt well with the demands of the twins; and on the odd occasion, he'd been excellent with Yvette.

Poor Yvette. Zoe shuddered.

"Hey," Jack kissed her, bringing her from her thoughts, "you alright?"

It still haunted her. She'd screamed: the nightmare had seemed so real. Jack couldn't calm her down alone, not without Tom and Kim's help. Poor Yvette had died, and they had taken Austin under their wing as she'd promised, only he too had taken his own life. They'd been destined to always be together, and he wasn't about to let her down now.

It had been so horribly realistic, Zoe couldn't be convinced at first that it was a nightmare. She'd opened the door, and Austin was there, Yvette's limp body cradled in his arms, heavy rain soaking them, although Austin was so tormented he barely acknowledged the storm.

That image haunted her: Austin's absent expression as he sat, on the edge of the sofa, in complete numb shock, inconsolable and unreachable. He stopped his medication, taking an overdose to help things along. She'd found him there: gone.

Zoe shook. She jumped as Jack cuddled her tightly. "It was so real..." She wept against him.

Jack was puzzled. It was understandable, but Yvette was so much stronger these days. Sure, it had taken many months, but she was back on an even keel.

So much so, she and Austin were in discussion of adopting again, their first had been many years previously. Their circumstances had changed in the last few years: now Austin too could be labelled with a chronic illness, it was another red flag against them.

What if something were to go drastically wrong? It wouldn't be the first time that they'd fallen ill, both of them. Jack had been involved in their talks, but didn't voice his thoughts, knowing it would break their friends' hearts. Time would tell.

Kim and Rob's relationship progressed when they could have some peace and quiet, which wasn't very often. It was surreal that he insisted they keep their underwear on, but also reassuring. She relaxed much more, knowing there was nothing to go wrong. Touching him was mind-blowing: he throbbed, she could actually feel the pulses, and it excited her. Kim's heart began to beat faster. They'd been going out for just over a year. She was nearly 16, nearly legally old enough. But was she ready?

Their friends were on another partner and all over them; it seemed like some of them had more boyfriends/girlfriends than they'd had hot dinners. But she and Rob were still together.

His eighteenth birthday was approaching fast. This was a special birthday and she had decided she wanted their first time to be that night.

Jack frowned at his teenagers again. "Now, are you sure you know where everything is?"

Kim and Tom nodded.

"And Tom, you will look after your sister, won't you?" Zoe cut in.

Kim rolled her eyes. "Mum, I can look after myself."

"Of course I will." He winked at Kim.

"Any wild parties..."

"...make sure you can't tell and that the place is spotless

when you come back on Tuesday. Yes, yes, we know." They both said in unison.

Jack and Zoe smiled, kissing their eldest offspring goodbye. Carly and Ryan were disappointed to be leaving their big brother and sister behind, and didn't understand why they couldn't stay too. Or why were they not coming?

Kim's plans for Rob's 18th that same weekend weren't going well. His parents were holding a surprise party - she'd wanted a night of peace. After all, this was the night. Excitement ran through her.

"Shhh!" They giggled together.

They'd escaped to his room, locking the door behind them; supplies already prepared and they were both ready. He was exciting her so much, her moaning was getting louder and louder. As much as he didn't want to curtail her fun, he felt he had to shush her.

"Everyone'll know what's happening."

They both laughed some more.

"Rob, I want you." Kim whispered, the smile lighting up her face.

Wow! How long had he waited to hear her say those words? His heart began to hammer; he continued to tease her with his fingers. There was only one problem: he didn't know how. Well, he did, but he'd never done this before: neither of them had. Inspiration struck him...

"Oh!" They both said, simultaneously.

Kim had a fleeting thought, but she dismissed it, of course he was using protection, she didn't know what it felt like with or without.

He moaned, his body shuddering and he lay panting on top of her. "I'm sorry, I couldn't help it."

She tried to hide her disappointment. But... "Could you do it again?" She stretched down to rub him, brushing against her own body, feeling where they were "joined". It was a wonderful feeling.

As he moved, she told him what felt good and what didn't, the feeling was building again. Oh yes, the orgasm wave was building up... she moaned, a long low moan.

Suddenly he pulled away. Kim opened her eyes. "I almost forgot!"

Quickly he changed the condom and lay back on the bed again. They could hear the party continuing downstairs.

"I'm sorry. You were almost there. But I couldn't go on."

"No, it's okay." Her heart was pounding. What if he'd... oh God, and if it had burst, or split open... or...

"Can we do it again? Are you okay?"

Kim smiled at him, kissing him as her answer.

It seemed within no time at all he was erect again and this time it was easier. She couldn't describe it. There were no proper words to describe the euphoria.

This time they climaxed together quickly, fast and hard, and lay locked together while they got their breath back. Giggling again as they cuddled, it felt strange to force themselves to get up and get dressed again in order to reappear at the party downstairs.

Hopefully nobody had taken much notice of their absence...

Chapter 26

Austin suggested getting away for a while when they were turned down, their respective illnesses preventing them from adoption.

It was a difficult decision to swallow, having spent so long discussing it and finally agreeing to apply. They had done a good job the first time, but there was no point in arguing. Sometimes watching the interactions between Zoe and Jack with their brood aroused painful jealousy pangs.

The couple headed to London for some time away, just the two of them. The first thing they did was buy another camera as Austin had plans for all the tourist attractions, including the lovely gardens and parks, and he too was determined to photograph their adventures.

Shopping and sightseeing were also on the agenda. It had been years since they'd lived in London, and it would be interesting to see how the big city had changed in their absence.

When the five-a-side season started again, Bob invited Austin back. The Premiers had failed in their challenge for promotion over the last few seasons, and now the gauntlet was thrown down again. Strengthening the team, Bob had some younger legs on the bench, desperate for the promotion he knew they deserved.

Helen and Yvette fussed over Phil when he suffered a nasty blow to the face during their first match. Austin switched, finding himself in goal for the first time in his career. Surely it wasn't that hard? It was widely acknowledged that the position of keeper was one of the least envied on the field.

It was a thought that hit home hard as he misjudged the ball and received it in the stomach, knocking the wind from him. From his crouched position, he indicated he was alright, though play stopped.

Yvette believed that the sugar rush he got from those barley sugars just about evened him out again, and was on hand at their break. Helen had Phil out of sight in their back room, his face already bruised and swollen. It wasn't a good start to the season: Phil out, and their new centre, James, already rattled. By the end, they had a nil-nil draw to show for their battle scars.

Austin was covered in scrapes and burns where he'd met the floor, diving to save the numerous goal attempts. That evening's shower was punctuated with yelps.

"You poor soul, you did ever so well too." Yvette was giving him sympathy.

Austin jumped, unaware that she was in the bathroom with him. "You took me by surprise, I didn't know you were here."

He could see that she was intent in staying where she was; in fact, she had the towel in her hands. It was so silly to find himself embarrassed by her presence. He was trapped, there was no way of getting out without her seeing him completely naked.

"Are you coming out or not? I'll be careful." She read the look in his eyes and frowned. "I can't remember the last time I saw you naked Austin, but I'm sure nothing's changed, nothing frightening anyway. Now come here, you'll get cold."

She hold the towel towards him, and he slid back the doors to step out, immediately wrapped in fluffy warmth: wincing as it rubbed his grazed elbows. Yvette was still looking at him. He reached for another towel, pulling her into his lap and wrapped it around both of them. She laughed from within his hold and he kissed her.

"I do love you, Yvette."

"Aww. I love you, Aus. More than words can say." She closed her eyes, revelling in the wonderful feeling of being held close to him. A sigh slipped out; a sigh of happiness. Austin's smile widened. He'd dreaded she would feel left out as the years went by and they met new people, worried that she would somehow penalise herself for not being normal. She was certainly a fighter, tougher than anyone he knew.

"Should we have an early night?" She suggested.

"Mmm," he agreed, kissing her neck. "You're so nice and warm." He gave her a gentle squeeze. "Who could refuse an invitation like that?"

He cuddled into her, allowing her to fall asleep first. Though she wouldn't admit it, the football wore her out: whether it was the worry over him, or the general pace he couldn't comprehend.

Her body was soft and warm, her breathing gentle and heartbeat steady. All these little checks he performed automatically now before allowing his mind to shut down for the night.

Chapter 27

"Sub me at half time."

Bob's eyes narrowed with suspicion. "Alright, what's going on?" He'd noticed Yvette was off-colour.

"I just want to make sure Eve's okay, that's all."

"Should you be here?"

Austin shrugged. "She's okay, I've checked. I've just got this feeling I should play half, that's all."

Phil had been back for a few matches and James was achieving good results at the front: so much so, Austin had begun to feel he wasn't needed. Well, that wasn't technically true; he was their troubleshooter. And he'd passed on some skills and hints to the team.

"We'll start without you, but you might be needed in the second half."

"Fine." Austin walked back to Yvette, immediately cuddling her when he sat down beside her. He could sense something wasn't right, but he couldn't put his finger on the problem. Neither could Yvette.

They watched as the team suffered a dreadful first half, and were down three-nil by the half time whistle!

"This is how last year went." Helen said, shaking her head. "This was the start of it."

It was nearly time for the top teams to go head-to-head in the quarter finals, and the next two results would determine whether the Premiers would be in or out.

"Be careful." Yvette whispered as Austin kissed her before getting up to go on.

He looked into her eyes and saw what he saw he didn't like the look of, yet Yvette was adamant she was fine. He stroked her cheek, relieved to find it was cool to his touch. When he looked over before the second half starting whistle, Helen had hooked his jumper over her shoulders and was sitting closer to her. His stomach flipped... and the ball smacked him in the head. It was a wake up call, he had to just get on with it and get this match over with.

"Right," he signalled to his team mates the plan and began to run.

Bob could hardly believe his eyes, sure that the eventual draw was nothing short of miraculous. 4-4 made an exciting storyline!

Austin abandoned his position within the celebrating team, quickly leaving the floor. Helen was the first to notice their absence, and worried she wouldn't be able to find them. Anxiously searching, she eventually tracked them down: Austin had ducked into the back, away from everyone; she found them in the quiet.

Finding him in tears, Yvette cradled in his arms, Helen's heart began to race. "Austin, what's wrong?"

"My poor Yvette. She's having a fit."

"A what?"

Austin tapped the side of his head.

"Shouldn't we lie her down?"

"That doesn't matter. She needs me." He spoke softly.

Helen felt more than confused. Austin looked tired and tearful, but quite calm and in control. It hit her then just how much he had to deal with, being her full time carer. It was no wonder that she always came first.

She jumped when he said her name. "Yes?"

Austin gave her a small smile. "Could you take us home, please, like last time?"

"Sure, of course. You don't need to take her to a doctor, or the hospital?"

Austin shook his head. "I know it seems strange. We can't do anything, not even at the hospital. It's best if we go home and I stay with her. She loses awareness for a while, but she's not in any danger."

Helen's heart leapt into her mouth, putting her hand up to her mouth. "Oh God, how awful!"

"I'm sorry, it's been a while since this has happened. It panics me a bit." He gave more of a grimace than a smile.

"I'm not surprised." Helen shook her head sympathetically. Yvette looked like she was asleep, apart from the shaking. She left them briefly as she made arrangements with Bob to take them home.

Bob had been livid at Austin's sudden departure, but soon forgot his anger. They'd done so well today and if they could stop the other team from scoring in their next match, they were in the playoffs. He needed Austin.

Zoe stopped at the doorway, seeing there were two strangers in the room with her friends. They looked up at her, and smiled.

"Sorry, we haven't met, have we? I'm Helen and this is Bob, my husband. You must be Zoe."

Zoe frowned, confused as to how they knew her yet she didn't know them. She nodded, unable to talk, too choked up. She linked her arm through Austin's, aware he was still in his shirt. Then it clicked who the couple were.

"Oh no, it happened at the game?" Horror resounded in her voice.

"Yes, but Austin knew straight away, and I took them home." Zoe nodded at Helen's words. "Poor Eve," she turned to Austin, "it's been so long. Why did it happen?"

He shrugged.

"We're here for you, Eve." She told her, automatically

reaching out to stroke Yvette's hair.

It struck her how peaceful she looked, so serene... and how much she looked just like she was asleep, when she wasn't twitching or moaning. Zoe fought the urge to cuddle her friend, aware of Bob and Helen's departure not long afterwards.

Bob was relieved to get a call from Austin the next week, also relieved to see him smiling. Like Helen, he too hadn't the faintest idea how Austin coped with it all.

"Eve's good, she came round in no time really."

"Ah, good." Bob sighed with relief. "But you won't be leaving her, not so soon?"

Austin shook his head, he gave Yvette on his lap a squeeze.

"No, sorry Bob, it's best not to count on me yet. Maybe in a few weeks."

"Don't worry, we'll see how you go." Bob gave him a kind, sympathetic smile. "Look after yourselves and keep in touch."

"Okay, thanks."

Once he'd disconnected the call, Yvette nuzzled into him more if that was possible. Austin responded by kissing her, and pulling the duvet around them. He felt tired himself, glad Yvette was settling down for an early night.

It was strange how much it took out of her; every time he worried she'd relapse before she got a chance to recuperate. But the fits were lessening: Zoe was right, Yvette had been fit-free for a long while before this. Encouragingly, her recovery time had picked up pace.

"You alright?" he whispered, kissing her head.

"Yeah." She was able to whisper back, just.

"Sleep sweetheart, I'm not far behind you."

Yvette smiled faintly, drifting off, nestled securely against him - safe, warm and loved.

Chapter 28

As they gathered together with the Premiers, they could feel the excitement growing, the atmosphere was positively buzzing. They were so close! Three wins from the promotion that every team member dreamed of. The only problem was that the other team, the Wanderers, were in exactly the same position - there was a fight to be had.

Bob reiterated the game plan to go easy before he left them to it for a few minutes before the starting whistle. Austin laid down their plans: Bob's "go easy" meant no rash tackles, no injuries and bust-a-gut performance. He wanted a lay up front first of all on the first whistle; that would set the tempo, he grinned. The guys all grinned too. He winked at Yvette and Helen, getting ready just off the centre marking, to Kev's left.

"He's got something planned," Yvette said, recognising that devious look on his face.

Helen frowned. "What d'you mean, Eve?"

"I don't know. We'll see."

Bob had a different formation for tonight - Phil in goal, Steve in defence, Kev in central, Austin and James up front.

"What the..." Bob didn't even get to finish before the ball was thumped over the line, past their opponents and into the goal, rebounding back out with almost as much pace.

Helen and Yvette laughed.

"That must be the quickest yet!" Helen exclaimed.

Austin was performing his trademark celebration - standing with one hand in the air, his first finger in the air: Numero Uno. Everyone laughed, even the team members who were jumping for joy on top of him.

And so the opposition concentrated on blocking Austin, thus allowing James to show off and shoot. Basically that was what the Premiers were doing – showing off. Bob shook his head in disbelief, going to sit with Helen and Yvette. Both looked at him, puzzled.

"I'm watching from here. They don't need me!" He explained, making them laugh.

It was a strangely reassuring sound, the squeaking of shoes on the polished wooden surface. Yvette closed her eyes, revelling in it.

"Kev!" James controlled the ball, and blatantly flicked it over the Wanderers' defence, to Andy who arrived a touch too late but managed to soon wrestle the ball off his opposite number and shot for glory.

Three-nil, in fifteen minutes!

A fortnight later, Bob was hoping for a similar result, but he knew this match would be a lot tougher. The opposition had a strange name; the Walkers "will walk all over you!" as the supporters chanted.

Bob's Premiers had a small following, but the noise from the Walkers' crowd of supporters was horrific in the enclosed space.

This was an away draw, in the next town, not so far from home. The box they had was unbreakable glass fronted, with a door cut into the side. The opposition's box next door and the supporter's area was also glass-fronted but roofless, hence the noise. It looked like an ice hockey stadium, minus the ice.

"Hey Bob, I'd get your guys to put these on." The Walkers' Assistant Coach stuck his head in the door and dropped an armful of pads onto the dressing room floor. "We're the county's best ice hockey team - five-a-side's a breeze for us." He laughed, allowing the changing room door to bang closed behind him.

"Oh shit!"

"You didn't tell us they're ice hockey players?!"

"More than players," Phil moaned, "they're county champions!"

Bob held his hands up for silence in the hubbub, for once not getting what he asked for. The collective dismay in the team could be physically felt in the air.

"Do you know how dirty they are in ice hockey?!" Someone said.

"Guys, there's nothing we can do about it. We're here now. We'll just have to be careful." Austin picked up a selection of the pads, swearing silently to himself. He knew no fancy tricks would get them through tonight. He continued. "The best thing we can do is stay strong. Take any openings we get, stay alert and try to hold for a draw, then we can get them at home, right Bob?"

Bob nodded. "Right, Austin."

"How does that help?" Even Phil, who was usually so positive, was sceptical.

Austin had the answer ready. "Well, for starters, their supporters won't all fit in, and they've not played away from home much - when they have the results have been more favourable to their opponents. We've a good ref, he won't put up with any tricks."

He was pleased to see the guys nodding.

They trekked out beside him, shaking hands as usual courtesy before a match with players and managers.

"Where's your Assistant, Bob?" The management was two-fold on the Walkers' side.

"Erm..." Bob hesitated.

"That's Austin." A few of his team mates shoved him forward.

"Oh, a Playing Assistant, nice touch." They smiled sarcastically.

Austin couldn't help himself, he growled inside; if there was one thing he couldn't stand it was snobbish sarcasm.

"C'mon then, heads or tails?"

"Heads." Austin called.

It was a sign, the coin landed on heads. He beamed: exactly what they needed.

Bob began to inform them of the plan as each team clustered together before the start. "James, I want you to drop back a bit and let Austin lead..."

"No," Austin interrupted, "sorry Bob, I think I should drop back. They're expecting me up front, so it should throw them if only for a little while if I play a quieter part. Plus I'm best to drop back to help defend. James' legs are younger and quicker after all." He smiled at his younger counterpart.

"Right, okay, Assistant." Bob smiled. "Go on guys, go easy and be careful, I don't want any injuries. I know there may be some rough play tonight. Austin said it best, be alert. And before we go on, I'm proud of all of you. We've done so well to get this far, even if we don't go through from here."

"You don't think we're going to win, do you?" Everyone could hear disgust in Austin's voice as he challenged Bob.

"C'mon guys, let's get 'em." He led his team mates off, shaking his head.

Bob laughed as he took his seat by Helen and Yvette. "And he thinks that reverse psychology doesn't work!"

The Walkers' began to play out wide, a strange tactic the Premiers had never come across before. It was difficult to get involved and almost impossible to tackle because of the oval shape to the arena; the high walls a further sticking point.

"Bloody hockey players." Austin cursed as first Kev, then he was shoved in the back and had his ankles hacked. He felt ridiculous with all the padding on, but it soon became apparent why it was a good idea. Elbows and knees, and even one for "your whatsits" as one of the guys exclaimed.

The best way to get revenge would be to score, and to humiliate the Walkers in front of their home crowd, Austin knew. All he could hear was the sound of blood pounding in his ears, and their noisy fans, so he knew shouting instructions and names wouldn't work. He'd practised with the guys and hoped that they'd remember a few things and look dangerous, if nothing else.

With five minutes on the board, he had a relatively easy tap in for the Premiers' first goal. His trademark celebration gave him a chance to look towards their box, smiling at Yvette and Helen sitting beside Bob. Of course, this gave the Walkers ammunition, fuelling their already fiery playing style.

As the ball flew into the air, towards him, he could see out of the corner of his eye an opponent charging towards him. There was no time for any avoidance manoeuvres.

"Fucking hell!" Bob exclaimed.

Everybody winced as the two players clattered together.

Despite the hammering of her heart, Yvette was touched to see the whole team gather around Austin. Several of them grabbed hold of him when he tried to stand up and found he couldn't put enough weight on his leg to walk, never mind continue playing.

Bob made for the door, stopping to call Austin's sub, getting James to line up the penalty and rearranging the team. The other two subs came onto the floor to help escort

Austin off.

"I'm gonna be covered in bruises tomorrow morning." He joked lightheartedly, taking hold of Yvette's hand as he sat heavily in the chair beside hers. "Something in my knee went." He answered the question posed to him about how he felt.

"I'm an ex-physio if you need a hand." A friendly voice said from their door.

"Oh yes, please." Helen said, looking up and smiling.

He didn't wear the opposition's shirt they were all thankful to see. "I'm Des, from the centre. I'm always needed at these matches." He made a face before turning to Austin. "I would suggest coming to the treatment room if you can. What is it, knee or ankle?"

Austin spoke between gritted teeth.

Des nodded. "It'll hurt, but we have to get that padding off somehow." He helped Austin down the corridor, recommending they go alone.

Yvette was a bag of nerves until she saw him hobbling back to them, ten very long minutes later.

He smiled. "What did I miss? Did James score?" Sinking slowly into the seat at the front of their box by her again, he squeezed Yvette's hand reassuringly.

"Yes, he scored, not much else happening - what's the diagnosis?" Bob had a bad feeling about this before he'd even heard the reply, seeing Austin's knee was wrapped in ice.

"I've never seen such swelling. It's difficult to say what really happened "

"Oh, Aus!" Yvette was horrified, cuddling into him.

He leant over, kissing her. "Don't worry Eve, I'll be okay. It just might take time."

Des appeared again, pulling Bob over to one side to

explain the ins and outs, knowing Austin was playing down the pain. He'd explained briefly of his home situation and Des had agreed.

"You're one star down for the final, I hope you've got a good back-up plan."

Bob paled. "Not as good as my star striker I haven't."

"Shame. I'd have him checked in a week, I wouldn't be surprised if it's ligament damage."

Bob winced. He'd suffered the same injury himself in his playing days.

Almost everyone in the stand applauded: Phil had made an outstanding save, just as the final whistle went. The players were all jumping for joy, but Bob could only manage a smile. Yes, they were through, with young James and Ali to lead them. There would be no chance for Austin now. He could've wept for the cruelty of the moment.

"You're getting used to coming back to ours, aren't you?" He could hear Austin joking with Helen. "Someone'll get the wrong idea one of these days."

Bob joined the conversation, laying his hand on Austin's shoulder.

"Ow!" Austin winced. "Probably grazed, only problem with playing on wooden surfaces."

"Sorry,"

"Don't worry, it's okay." He caught Bob's expression as the team filtered off to get changed.

Sorrowfully, Bob shook his head. "I'm sorry Austin, I didn't want you to get injured."

"Hey, it wasn't your fault."

"You know you won't be fit to play?"

"Very likely." Austin squeezed Yvette's hand. "I'm too old to fight these things off any more." He joked, smiling faintly. "Go congratulate them. You can tell them I'm sidelined, but we'll be here to see them win."

Austin related the tale to Helen and Yvette of how Des had been forced to cut the padding off because of the swelling. He could feel it was lessening, little by little, but knew there was no way he'd be fit for the final, even if it were in a month.

His knee had been weakened during his original playing days with Jack, in fact both of his knees had suffered, and that on top of Yvette's injuries had forced his retirement.

Chapter 29

"We can't do it without you." Ali said, speaking for the team. Austin had sent Bob away while they talked before the match. "You can't have given up already? Before you get out there and measure up the opposition?" "You're our best player. You set things up. You make goals and you help us defend." Kev continued.

Austin shrugged. "No one person wins a team event. And nobody is invincible, right?" He got no response from this. "If you were to leave your jobs, would your bosses sit down and moan that the business wouldn't run?"

He received many puzzled looks.

"No, of course not, he gets a replacement - and though that replacement doesn't know the job as well as you did, he gets it done. He works hard for the business and ensures success, right?"

"Right..." Came the wary collective answer.

"Right. So get out there and work as a team. You've all done well, I never thought we'd get this far, but we did it. You know this is Bob's dream: he's desperate for promotion. We've done this for him, and for ourselves. Think how proud you all felt when you went home last week. How the wife let you sit down and poured you a drink."

They all laughed.

"You play the game and you take your chances in this world. You only have one life, okay, make the most of it. Do what you enjoy doing and give it your all. Never look back and think what if...?

We can do this. We're here, aren't we? We defeated the favourites, all season we proved ourselves. And I tell you something, we're favourite to win tonight."

Austin let this sink in, able to see his talk working.

"Promise me something guys. Promise us you'll do your best; you'll go out there and you'll be the best."

Bob beamed widely from his position on the other side of the door, having heard every word. He was impressed. Firstly last week, when his team mates had pushed him forward for Assistant, and now.

As the team filtered out and onto the floor, Bob paused. He heard Austin groan from behind the door, opening it to find him entangled in metal crutches.

"Bloody things," he laughed, seeing Bob looking at him.

"While you're still here." He threw him a shirt, which Austin caught, glad of the excuse to rid himself of the metal supports for a few minutes longer.

"What's this?"

"I want you to put it on." Bob went back into the dressing room, and sat down beside him.

Austin looked at him puzzled, unfolding the shirt. He caught his breath as he saw the embroidered script on the chest: Austin Leigh, Premiers Assistant Coach

"Oh no, I can't."

"Yes, you can." Bob was unsure of Austin's reaction, and glad when a slow smile spread across his face. "The guys and I, we thought it was only right." His smile widened when he realised Austin was too choked to speak. "Game starts in a few minutes. I'll see you in the box."

Austin nodded, wallowing in his moment.

"Well done you." Yvotte whispered, cuddling him. She could see how much this meant to him. "Just a shame you can't get up there."

"What's done is done, and what's buggered is buggered. And I'm definitely buggered." The four laughed.

Fortunately he was able to do most things, although it was best to make use of the supports while they were out, precautionarily. This, at least, was his excuse for getting tangled up!

Their opposition were the Coast Crawlers, no prizes for guessing where they were based. Bob noted the local sports journalist was present, with a staff photographer. The Premiers had become increasingly newsworthy by the closing stages of the competition.

Tonight if the score stayed equal, it came down to a sudden death penalty shoot out. Austin had been most insistent on hanging on for a draw and going to penalties, and had bored them into a shoot out drill. Bob laughed to himself, wondering if Austin had known the result of the match before it had even started?

It was slow and boring, even Bob had to admit, so much so half time was a blessing. He went into the dressing room alone. They came out minutes before the second half, coming past the box. Austin's expression said it all, and he nodded at them, they all nodded back.

Kev let out a blast that any striker would've been proud of, and that seemed to wake the Coasters up - suddenly they were one-nil down. They began to move like the equaliser was in their grasp. Bob and Austin winced as the ball went in the back of their net. And again.

Austin got up, making his way haphazardly to the line, whistling and gesturing. Everyone looked stunned, except the Premiers; they nodded and digested this information.

Their formation changed. Onlookers became more puzzled, especially as the ball was allowed down the side with ease and almost to the box. Steve borrowed Austin's favourite trick, a nutmeg through the opponent's legs, and sent the ball up to Kev.

The Coasters had only their defenders in their half, and James and Ali began to run. The opposition almost caught up, one getting tangled with Ali to send them both flying, while James took his opportunity to take on the keeper. James swept past their keeper for another equaliser. He may have been the baby of the bunch, in his late twenties, but those younger legs were the boost the team needed at times. Like this.

"What the hell did you say to them?" Bob was amazed.

Austin smiled. "If I told you, I'm afraid I'd have to kill you." He joked.

The referee blew for full time, and turned to the coaches. It would be the best of three, after a fifteen minute break. They were told to make their choices.

Austin rattled off three of their players, in the order he wanted them, immediately. Bob was aghast: he had a vague idea of who would work best. It was a pressure issue and he was puzzled by Austin's choice.

"Now, don't get me wrong, Ali's good, but I know Phil deals with pressure best. I want him to start. Then Kev has a bit of a cushion, then I want James to finish us off."

"Why Kev, then James?" Bob quizzed him.

"Kev can do it if he controls himself, but if we need to rely on the third man, then James will do it for us."

"I don't understand," Helen said, "why Phil?"

"Because Phil understands how the penalty is taken." Yvette said, aware that all eyes were on her. "I'm getting used to this." She said by way of explanation.

Austin smiled and squeezed her hand, kissing her. "You're good."

"Thank you." She replied, kissing him back. "Either that or I've been a footballer's wife too long."

"That sounds familiar." Helen agreed, smiling at them both.

There was laughter from the crowd as Phil stepped up for the first crack at goal. The Crawlers' keeper looked confused to be facing his opposite number.

Phil took a run up... and chipped it over the keeper's head, into the back of the net. The grin nearly split his face as his team mates jumped all over him, as tradition led. He pulled away, looking over at the box, and made Austin's celebration gesture.

Tension began to build.

The Crawler's most experienced player stepped up to take their first penalty, which Phil missed by the tip of his fingers. In fact, he stood where he was, his fingers clamped tightly in his other hand. That hurt.

Kev nervously got hold of the ball and slowly made his way to the spot. Silence fell. He looked over and Austin caught his eye, nodding and pointing first at him, then at James and shrugging his shoulders. Kev smiled: Austin was right, it didn't matter if he didn't score, because James was a sure bet. Still...

His hands shook as he positioned the ball. Taking a few deep breaths and stepping back a few paces, the goal seemed so much smaller from here. He decided on shooting straight down the middle, remembering how the keeper always went either right or left. It was a game of chance, after all.

The whistle blew and he went for it. Ali's shout broke through his subconscious, and he hugged his new strike partner, unable to believe he'd scored!

Phil was still flexing his sore fingers as he stood on the line, watching the second of the opposition lining up. He noticed the man was a left-footer and smiled to himself, he could guess this one.

And guess correctly he did. The ball sailed through the air and Phil got his hand to it, punching it safely out of harm's way. Safely, but painfully. He could feel his fingers inside the glove swell.

The home crowd were yelling and screaming, but it wasn't over yet. The teams still had one player each: the title was yet to be secured. Phil gestured to Helen as if to wrap up his hand; she nodded and tossed him the tape. This was worrying. There was no subbing to be done. If it affected his performance...

James laughed, playfully bowing to the crowd when they called his name, before taking his place. They were all so sure that he'd do it... but it was a different kettle of fish here, standing here in front of the crowd alone, just you and the keeper, one on one. He recalled the words of his coach: "Take your time and concentrate." Bob had told him.

"Do what feels right." Austin had added to Bob's good sense advice.

He knew the keeper would get to the ball, it was only a small goal after all, and they knew each other well: they used to practice together until this final match. Not that anyone knew they were friends. He swallowed hard.

Well, Austin had said do what felt right: he felt like hitting it as hard as he could, and straight at the keeper, so that was what he did. Straight into his hands.

A gasp came up from the crowd. Bob and Austin groaned simultaneously: the Premiers team had their heads in their hands.

Phil trudged to the goal. He was a ridiculous sight, having strapped his middle and index fingers together. The penalty was taken quickly and bounced off his chest, rebounding almost back to the striker, who let rip another shot which was perfectly allowed.

Every muscle stretching, he managed to tip the shot over the bar, losing his balance and falling into the goal. His team mates piled on top of him.

Books by Yvonne Marrs

Introduction to the Fictional Work of Yvonne Marrs

When The Sax Man Plays Part 1 - Making It

When The Sax Man Plays Part 2 - Proving It

When The Sax Man Plays Part 3 - Managing It

When The Sax Man Plays Part 4 - His Return

When The Sax Man Plays Part 5 - The Prequel

When The Sax Man Plays ...and All That Jazz

Football Crazy 1: A World Cup Adventure

Football Crazy 2: On The Edge of Glory

Football Crazy 3: The Hat-trick

Football Crazy 4: A Point to Prove

Football Crazy 5: The Master of Managerial Psychology

Aiden Lewis Octet Book 1 - Memoirs

Aiden Lewis Octet Book 2 - Reminiscence

Aiden Lewis Octet Book 3 - Touring

Aiden Lewis Octet Book 4 - Bravado

Aiden Lewis Octet Book 5 - Partnership

Aiden Lewis Octet Book 6 - Vulnerable

Aiden Lewis Octet Book 7 - Struggles

Aiden Lewis Octet Book 8 - Denouement

Undeserved 1

Undeserved 2

Undeserved 3

Putting The Visible Into So-Called Invisible Illnesses
Through Poetry

Castiliano Vulgo - An Elizabethan Story

Harbourtown Murder

Inexorable

Termination at the Halt

Can't Buy Health 1

Can't Buy Health 2

Can't Buy Health 3

Can't Buy Health 4

Can't Buy Health 5

Can't Buy Health 6

Can't Buy Health 7

Can't Buy Health 8

We hope you have enjoyed this book,
please leave a review for Yvonne.

Here are a few other links you might like:

Yvonne's Site

Yvonne's Blog

The World of Yvonne Marrs Facebook page

Printed in Poland
by Amazon Fulfillment
Poland Šp. z o.o., Wrocław

94305985R00085